A THEOLOGICAL POSITION

Also by Robert Coover

The Origin of the Brunists

The Universal Baseball Association, Inc.
J. Henry Waugh, Prop.

Pricksongs & Descants

Robert Coover
A
Theological
Position

Plays

THE KID

LOVE SCENE

RIP AWAKE

A THEOLOGICAL POSITION

E. P. DUTTON & CO., INC. | NEW YORK | 1972

Published simultaneously in Canada
by Clarke, Irwin & Company
Limited, Toronto and Vancouver
Library of Congress Catalog Card Number: 77-158593
SBN 0-525-216006 (Cloth)   SBN 0-525-045406 (Paper)

"The Kid" first appeared in *Tri-Quarterly 18* (Spring 1970).
"Love Scene" first appeared in *New American Review 12* (1971).

For Elaine May, Nancy Duncan,
John Lahr, and Gail Goodwin,
in respectful thanks
for helping bring this book
of acts about.

Contents

THE KID

CHARACTERS

The Kid
The Sheriff
The Deputy
A Barkeep and several
Cowpokes and Belles

Inside an Old West frontier town saloon. BARKEEP *and ten to twelve* COWPOKES: *four or five playing poker at a big table, another five or six drinking at the bar, others scattered, reading papers, dozing, etc. Among the men at the bar are* THE SHERIFF *and his* DEPUTY. THE SHERIFF *is one of those soft-spoken goodguy worrier types from the Western flicks, average height and build, about forty or so, the kind who is always rubbing his jaw thoughtfully, gazing off, waiting and praying that the Marshall will turn up, a little clumsy, ingenuous, modest, yet heroic and dependable. His* DEPUTY *is skinny, amiable, a little goofy, maybe an older gent. The rest of the men in the town saloon are the usual run of Western extras, generally a little swarthy, beardy, slovenly in dull gray and brown cowboy duds, none of them looking too trustworthy. Lights or curtain*

*can go up on a tableau (cards about to be dealt, drinks
about to be drunk, foot about to be raised to the rail, etc.),
set into motion by some signal (e.g., the swinging doors
suddenly slapping open, or gunfire, or the amplified crack
of a playing card): noisy hubbub of drinks being ordered,
stories being told, arguments being waged, drinks sliding
along the bar, betting of cardplayers, etc., interrupted almost immediately by the breathless arrival, through the
swinging doors, of three or more dance-hall ladies, all called*
BELLE. *Sudden silence and all eyes—except* THE
SHERIFF's—*on them. (The* BELLE *and* COWPOKE *lines,
here numbered consecutively for convenience, should be
passed out randomly enough to make it difficult to distinguish the character of one* BELLE *or* COWPOKE *from another. In fact, they may, if they wish, trade off lines in different performances; each line has its essential character
and place, and it shouldn't matter who delivers it. Clarity,
control, and a fairly fast pace [no ad-libbing!] are essential
to the play.) In all that follows, the girls reveal—clicking
their heels, whirling their skirts, rubbing their hips, and so
on—a mounting sexual excitement, their lines delivered
to the world, not the* COWPOKES.

BELLE 1 : He's comin! I seen him!

BELLE 2 : Out on the flats!

BELLE 3 : Stirrin up the dust, boys!

BELLE 4 : Stirrin up the wind!

BELLE 5 : Clappin mean spurs tuh his big red roan!

BELLE 6: Movin acrost the desert like a wild blue eagle!

BELLE 7: Movin acrost the grasslands like white lightnin!

BELLE 8: Splittin the breeze! Pourin it on! Ridin like all forty, boys!

BELLE 9: Like a bat outa hell, boys!

BELLE 10: Like all possessed!

BELLE 11: Good Lord! He's *beautiful!*

Since the moment the girls burst into the saloon, the COWPOKES *have been motionless, apprehensive yet calm, silent, as though poised for action. Some of those seated have half risen, and the men at the bar have swung about to give full attention to the ladies—all but* THE SHERIFF *whose back is turned still, and* THE DEPUTY *who is watching* THE SHERIFF. *Now, one of the men breaks in:*

COWPOKE 1: *Who*, Belle? *Who* did yuh say was comin?

BELLE 12: The *Kid*, hombre! *The Kid's comin!*

Now THE SHERIFF *does turn from the bar, slowly, as though troubled, weary, yet alert, hands coming to rest lightly on the butts of his two holstered six-shooters. He seems to be mulling over what he's just heard, thinking things out, looking at the girls, yet gazing beyond them. He flexes his hands, rubs them absently on his hips and holsters.* THE DEPUTY, *now staring at the* BELLES *in open-mouthed wonderment, lets his glass slip through his shaking hand*

and crash to the floor (slightly amplified). The other men in the saloon turn to THE SHERIFF, *most of them in dead seriousness, as though perhaps waiting for him to make a move, issue commands, lead them forth—but two or three* COWPOKES *seem about to erupt into laughter. One of these latter, suppressing a grin, says with great feeling:*

COWPOKE 2: Oh no! Not the Kid!

DEPUTY: Gosh all willikers!

BELLE 13: Yes, the Kid, damn it! Ridin tall and easy in the saddle through the great clean silence!

BELLE 14: Yes, strikin sharp spurs tuh his lean wire-tough chestnut, boys, and burnin up the prairie!

BELLE 15: Wingin it over the ridges at a long swingin lope, big hands clamped hard on the reins!

BELLE 16: Hands big on the pommel, boys!

BELLE 17: Ridin hard in the saddle!

BELLE 18: In the saddle, boys! Sweet in the saddle!

BELLE 19: Pushin that big silver stallion, hot from wranglin dogies in the Badlands!

BELLE 20: From runnin broomtails and bustin broncs!

BELLE 21: Bustin banks, boys!

BELLE 22: Jammin hot spurs in the flanks a that Barb!

BELLE 23: Packin the mail!

BELLE 24: Oh, he's fleet as a deer, boys, and tougher'n a mule!

BELLE 25: Yes, and purty as a pitcher!

BELLE 26: And he's nobody's fool, boys! He's nobody's fool!

DEPUTY: (*squeaking out in the silence*) No! No, he ain't!

> *This causes a light ripple of laughter among the* COWPOKES (THE SHERIFF. *is still silent, thoughtful, preoccupied), as the* BELLES *step forward to sing the ballad, "The Savior of the West," assisted by the* COWPOKES. *Some of the* COWPOKES *play guitars, harmonicas, banjos, fiddles, etc., or alternatively, they pretend to play them while the accompaniment is piped in electronically. Occasional "whoopee's" and "yahoo's."* THE DEPUTY *joins in on the first chorus, but he is loudly off key—one of the* COWPOKES, *grimacing at the noise, swats him playfully with his hat to shut him up. The* BELLES, *sharing the verses, may pass a handmike among them. Their performance is a cross between a dance-hall routine and country gospel singing: a hillbilly mix of sex, sentiment, and self-righteousness.*

THE SAVIOR OF THE WEST

Come hear the Kid's story,
It's bloody and gory,
And it's shore tuh put hair on yore chest!

He kin lick any man,
And he don't give a damn!
He's the Savior of the West!
  He's the Savior of the West!

He left eighty men dyin
Down south of the line,
And robbed sixteen trains of their gold!
Shed blood by the bucket,
Told the Marshall tuh fuck it,
Before he was twelve years old!
  Before he was twelve years old!

CHO: Yes, a gent or a dame,
  It's all the same
  Tuh the Kid when he puts em tuh rest!
  Cuz killin's his game,
  They all know him by name,
  He's the Savior of the West!
    He's the Savior of the West!

He's killt Apaches, Cayuses,
And Potawatami papooses,
And buggered the Chickasaw chiefs!
Rid the country of snakes,
And shit in the lakes,
And hung all the schoolmarms and thiefs!
  Hung all the schoolmarms and thiefs!

When the killin's all done,
They ain't anyone
Left standin 'cept fer the Kid!
He's the number one gun,
And fer him it's jist fun,
Surveyin all the dead!
  Surveyin all the dead!

CHO: Yeah, the Kid is his name,
And he's too tough tuh tame,
He's the fastest, the meanest, the best!
Jist blam! blam! blam!
And he don't give a damn!
He's the Savior of the West!
He's the Savior of the West!

Whooping and hollering after the song, shouts of "Amen!", "That's tellin it!", and so on, excited embraces. Then they all turn toward THE SHERIFF *and* THE DEPUTY. *They nod suggestively toward* THE SHERIFF, *apparently trying to remind* THE DEPUTY *of something.* THE SHERIFF *remains as before, gazing thoughtfully off.* THE DEPUTY *looks puzzled, then seems suddenly to remember.*

DEPUTY: Hey! Sheriff!

SHERIFF: Yeah?

DEPUTY: Sheriff, the Kid's hit town!

SHERIFF: Yeah . . . I know . . .

DEPUTY: Well, uh, whadda we gonna *do?*

SHERIFF: I dunno. (*Sighs.*) We'll do what we have tuh do, I reckon.

DEPUTY: (*swaggering a little*) Yuh mean we're gonna go after that mean lowdown nogood varmint, Sheriff?

SHERIFF: I figger we ain't got no choice. He's broke the law and he's hurt a lotta people.

DEPUTY: (*still swaggering*) Yup, I knowed that's what yuh'd say, and yuh know what?

SHERIFF: What?

DEPUTY: (*swagger collapsing*) I'm *skeered*, Sheriff!

SHERIFF: (*smiling gently, clapping a reassuring hand to his* DEPUTY'*s trembling shoulders*) Aw, c'mon now, podnuh! Y'ain't gonna let these jaspers here catch yuh in no lily-livered funk, are yuh?

DEPUTY: (*still quailing*) I reckon I ain't got no more choice about that than you got about chasin varmints, Sheriff!

THE SHERIFF *laughs loosely, then strides manfully toward the swinging doors. There, he turns, addresses the* COWPOKES *in the saloon. They listen attentively, a little guiltily at first (a practiced guilt: they've been through this before), then later with some (real) surprise. The* BELLES *turn their back on* THE SHERIFF.

SHERIFF: Men, I got somethin tuh say tuh yuh. It won't take long and it pains me some tuh talk of it, but I might never git another chance tuh speak tuh yuh like this, and I feel as how I gotta say it. (COWPOKES *seem a little uneasy, though some wink at each other.*) I'm shore yuh all know by now: the Kid's back in town. (*Some* COWPOKES *react as though getting the news for the first time.*) Now, I know what you're thinkin. You're thinkin, that goldurn Sheriff's gonna ask us tuh help him go after that ornery varmint. And yuh don't want tuh go. Nobody's ever outshot the Kid, and yuh don't wanna git killt. You're skeered. Well, I don't blame yuh none. I'm skeered, too. But you're wrong. I *ain't* gonna ask yuh to go with me! (*Mild surprise, artificial relief, some gathering consternation. The* BELLES, *curious, now turn to attend him.*) I ain't never told yuh this before, but, well, yuh see, this here star I'm wearin, it means a whole lot tuh me. Like a lotta you boys, I first come in tuh this here community with nuthin but the shirt on muh back and the hoss I was ridin . . . and even the damn hoss was half dead! (*This was meant as a joke, and* THE SHERIFF *pauses, smiling. A few* COWPOKES *chuckle awkwardly, glancing uneasily at each other.*) But this here town's been good tuh me, the folks here is decent and law-abidin, and it's a place where a man kin be his own man. And I wanna say, right here and now, I was mighty proud the day yuh all seen fit tuh make me yore Sheriff. Might seem like a mite small thing tuh some of yuh, but, men, I gotta tell yuh straight out so's yuh know how I feel: it's the greatest goldurn thing ever happened tuh me, and, well, like I say, I'm mighty damn proud. (THE SHERIFF *fingers his star thoughtfully, proudly.*) And so I been thinkin: what could I do tuh live up tuh this here badge? What could I do tuh live up tuh the trust you folks've put in me? And then it come tuh me. Sheriff, I says tuh myself, Sheriff, fer them: *you gotta face the Kid alone!*

COWPOKE 3: Uh, now hold up, Sheriff—

COWPOKE 4: They ain't no need tuh—

SHERIFF: No, boys! I done made up muh mind! It's me or the Kid!

COWPOKE 5: But—!

SHERIFF: (*fully worked up now*) No "buts" about it, boys! It's law and order has made this town great, and it's my job as Sheriff tuh see it's kep, that's what yuh elected me fer, that's why yuh give me this here badge, and I mean tuh do what's gotta be done!

> THE SHERIFF *wheels about and slaps his way out through the swinging doors before anyone can answer.* THE DEPUTY *blinks once at the* COWPOKES *in registration of his own astonishment, then squares his shoulders bravely, shoves down on his six-shooters with determination—and pushes the gunbelt right down off his hips, tripping over it as he attempts to follow* THE SHERIFF *out, falling to his face on the barroom floor. He jumps up sheepishly and staggers hurriedly out, trying to pull up his gunbelt as he stumbles along. Saloon erupts in full-bellied laughter. A couple* COWPOKES *leap up and dance a little impromptu jig with the* BELLES, *slapping them playfully on their behinds.*

COWPOKE 6: Hey, yuh don't think he's gonna screw it up, do yuh?

COWPOKE 7: Who, the Sheriff? Haw haw!

COWPOKE 8: I mean, he kinda got things crossed up there, like he—

COWPOKE 9: Deppity'll keep an eye on him!

COWPOKE 10: Hey, yuh got everything ready?

COWPOKE 11: Ready as she'll ever be!

> COWPOKE *11, holding one fist over his head, crossing his eyes, and lolling his tongue, does a little dance on his toes as though hanging himself, as another* COWPOKE, *off tune, sings a snatch of the final song:*

COWPOKE 12: Oh, the West was a place a grace and glory . . . !

> *General laughter.*

COWPOKE 13: This is gonna be good!

> *Whoopeeing and music-making is interrupted by a* COWPOKE *standing near the swinging doors, looking out.*

COWPOKE 14: Hey! *Here he comes!*

> Cowpokes *and* belles *fall rapidly into poses around tables, at the bar, etc. Total silence in the old saloon, as all wait breathlessly. In strides* THE KID. *He slaps the swinging doors hard as he enters, making* BELLES *and* COWPOKES *gasp and start. He is tall, blond, broad-shouldered, narrow-hipped, graceful, elegant. He might wear, for example, a white Stetson (brim flattened up cockily on the sides), white full-cuffed gloves, white gunbelt and boots, tight*

navy-blue shirt and pants, red kerchief around the neck. Bright silver six-shooters in white holsters, strapped low on his thighs. There might even be a special spot turned on him to give him additional radiance. He is, in short, a real impressive piece of magical meanness. He surveys the room, hands at hips. Tips back his hat with his thumb as he gazes defiantly at the COWPOKES, *his expression cold and humorless. He turns his steady gaze on* THE BAR-KEEP, *sweating motionlessly behind the bar.*

COWPOKE 15: Hey, uh, better pour the Kid a drink there, podnuh!

COWPOKE 16: Yeah, right! Hurry it up, Mac! The Kid's waitin!

COWPOKE 17: The Kid must be purty damn thirsty after his long ride!

COWPOKE 18: Thirsty! Right!

COWPOKE 19: Ain't that right, Kid?

Slowly, keeping his eye warily on THE KID, THE BARKEEP *is meanwhile setting a shotglass on the bar, filling it. Now, faster than the eye can see,* THE KID *draws and fires, blasting both shotglass and whiskey bottle with the same shot.* BARKEEP *grimaces, but doesn't flinch.* COWPOKES *and* BELLES *fall back, some taking cover. The gunblasts should be very loud, accompanied if possible by puffs of gunsmoke from the barrels; the sounds of shattering glass (and*

*all other sounds that follow) should be amplified.
To augment the illusion of* THE KID'S *speed, the
gunblasts should sound at virtually the same moment the guns are drawn from their holsters. Dia-
logue should move very fast, though each line
should be played for all it is worth. No mumbling
or vague crowd noises—all lines specific and
clear. Some of the lines may be distributed to*
BELLES, *if desired.*

COWPOKE 20: Whatsamatter? Yuh don't like that brand,
Kid?

COWPOKE 21: Reckon the Kid don't go fer that cheap kinda
whiskey, Mac!

COWPOKE 22: Reckon yuh better find somethin a little better!

COWPOKE 23: Somethin a little smoother!

COWPOKE 24: Reckon yuh better make it pronto, podnuh!

COWPOKE 25: Yuh don't fool around none with the Kid!

COWPOKE 26: By God, yuh *don't!*

THE BARKEEP, *keeping his eyes on* THE KID , *reaches
behind him for another bottle, but no sooner does
he pick it up than* THE KID *blasts it out of his hand.*
THE BARKEEP, *eyes narrowing, grabs up six or
seven bottles and sets them on the bar, then ducks
behind it.* THE KID, *firing rapidly, blasts away every
bottle but one.* THE BARKEEP's *hand appears, setting*

a new shotglass on the bar, but THE KID grabs up the
*remaining bottle, smashes its top off with a blow
against the bar, and chugalugs its contents. Meanwhile, this has been going on:*

COWPOKE 27: Hey! Did yuh see *that!*

COWPOKE 28: Shot up ever damn bottle but one!

COWPOKE 29: Jist blam blam, man!

COWPOKE 30: That Kid's got taste, podnuh!

COWPOKE 31: I reckon he *does!*

COWPOKE 32: Blam blam! Gawdamighty!

COWPOKE 33: Hey, I reckon he's some kinda drinker, too!

COWPOKE 34: Yuh betcha life, hombre! Lookit him go!

COWPOKE 35: Boys, they ain't nuthin the Kid cain't do better'n any ten men! (*Sudden blast from* THE KID'*s six-shooter—his free hand—though without a pause in his drinking, and this* COWPOKE'*s hat flies off. The other* COWPOKES *duck.*) Woops! Uh, make that *fifty* men!

COWPOKE 36: *Fifty* men okay, Kid?

COWPOKE 37: I say a *hunderd!*

COWPOKE 38: Hell, yes!

COWPOKE 39: How's a *hunderd*, Kid?

COWPOKE 40: Boy, he's *somethin!*

COWPOKE 41: Boy, *ain't* he!

THE KID *has been ignoring them, finishing off the whiskey. He now heaves the empty bottle away (amplified splintering crash of the bottle), wipes his mouth with the back of one white-gloved hand, and flatly, without expression, though perhaps faintly threatening:*

THE KID: Coma ti yi youpy youpy yea.

COWPOKE 42: Right! Hah! You bet, Kid! Whoopee.

COWPOKE 43: Youpy youpy yea, man!

COWPOKES *and* BELLES *all join in happy repetitions of* THE KID's *line, with variations. Brief silence follows. One* COWPOKE *(46) absently shuffles a deck of cards (amplified flutter of the shuffle).* THE KID *draws, fires a single blast, and a card flies out of the deck. The* COWPOKE *shakes his hand loosely from the wrist, blows on it, etc., as though it were burnt.*

COWPOKE 44: Whew! I reckon he didn't like yuh shufflin them cards!

COWPOKE 45: Reckon he didn't like yuh breakin the silence!

COWPOKE 46: S–s–sorry, Kid!

COWPOKE 47: The Kid's big on silence!

COWPOKE 48: You said it, podnuh!

COWPOKE 49: *Very* big!

COWPOKE 50: The biggest!

COWPOKE 51: What card did he shoot outa there?

COWPOKE 46: (*picking up the card and examining it; in wonder*) Jack a spades!

COWPOKE 52: How bout that! Jack a spades!

COWPOKE 46: (*again*) Shot him plumb through the left eye!

COWPOKE 53: Hey! Lemme see that!

> *He grabs the card, looks at it, passes it around. All admire it, whistle, show it to others, etc. One* BELLE *finally tucks it in her bodice or garter, casting long suggestive glances toward* THE KID. THE KID *makes a gesture with his six-shooter toward the* COWPOKE *(46) with the cards.*

COWPOKE 54: Hey! It looks like the Kid wants somethin!

COWPOKE 55: It looks like he's got somethin on his mind!

COWPOKE 56: Whadda yuh want, Kid?

COWPOKE 57: I git it! The Kid wants yuh tuh shuffle them cards agin!

COWPOKE 58: Yeah, that's it! Give em another riffle there, podnuh!

> *Watching* THE KID *warily, the* COWPOKE *(46) with the cards again sits at the table, picks up the deck, shuffles the cards loosely and loudly. Three fast gunblasts from* THE KID's *six-shooters, and three more cards fly from the deck.* COWPOKE *46 jumps*

up, kissing his hand, pressing it between his thighs, grimacing, etc., as other COWPOKES *and* BELLES *rush for the three cards. As they pick them up:*

COWPOKE 59: Jack a diamonds!

BELLE 27: Jack a hearts!

COWPOKE 60: Goddamn! Jack a clubs!

COWPOKE 61: Goddamn! He shot all three jacks clean outa there!

COWPOKE 62: Goddamn! That's somethin tuh *see!*

COWPOKE 63: You kin say yuh was *there*, podnuh!

COWPOKE 64: Shot all three goddamn jacks outa there!

BELLE 28: Four, hombre! Four!

COWPOKE 64: (*again*) Four! Goddamn right, Belle! All four!

BELLE 29: And hey! Lookit here, boys! He shot all four of em in the *left eye!*

COWPOKE 65: Goddamn! Drilled em neat as a pin!

COWPOKE 66: They's somethin the Kid don't cater to about *left eyes!*

COWPOKE 67: He ain't very big on *left eyes!*

COWPOKE 68: What yuh got agin *left eyes*, Kid?

COWPOKE 69: He's a lot bigger on silence!

COWPOKE 70: Jist blam blam, hombre! Holy shit!

THE KID: (*flatly, as before*) Youpy youpy ti yi youpy youpy yea.

> COWPOKES *and* BELLES *once more imitate* THE KID, *working variations on his line. Any variations will do, and they should all overlap chorally, but they should be celebrative, clear, and resonant, not mumbling or blurred. A man steps through the swinging doors—*THE KID *spins and fires eight or ten shots, dropping the stranger, who kicks and jerks with each shot.* COWPOKES *and* BELLES *rush excitedly over to examine the body. The* BELLES, *who have been throwing occasional coy glances toward* THE KID, *now begin to flirt more openly with him, but he pays absolutely no attention to them. He is completely self-absorbed, though his blue eyes are ever watchful.*

COWPOKE 71: Whew! That fella's suddenly about as dead as he's ever gonna be!

COWPOKE 72: Right smack in the *left eye!*

COWPOKE 73: And about ever place else tuh boot!

COWPOKE 74: Ain't enough fer the Kid jist tuh kill em, he's gotta tattoo em!

COWPOKE 75: Gotta sign his name! Haw haw!

COWPOKE 76: Boys, lemme tell yuh, they ain't *nobody* like the Kid!

COWPOKE 77: Hey, but who's the poor fuckin stranger?

COWPOKE 78: Hard tuh tell. Ain't all that much left of him!

COWPOKE 79: Hey, boys! It's the Marshall!

COWPOKE 80: Be damned if it ain't! Whew! Cain't hardly reckanize him after what the Kid done to him!

COWPOKE 81: Mebbe somebody oughta go tell the Sheriff!

COWPOKE 82: Whoa, man!

COWPOKE 83: Sshh! Yuh wanna git killt?

COWPOKE 84: Hoo boy! It shore don't pay tuh be no Marshall when the Kid's around!

COWPOKE 85: It shore ain't the happiest time tuh be a goddamn lawman, now when the Kid's in town!

BELLE 30: God in heaven! that was *beautiful*, boys! I'd like tuh see that agin!

COWPOKE 86: Yeah, but we ain't got no more Marshalls, Belle!

COWPOKE 87: Marshalls is gittin hard tuh come by!

> *During this scene, a couple* COWPOKES *should drag "the Marshall's" body out through the swinging doors. "The Marshall" may in fact be played by one of the* COWPOKES, *who has sneaked off the set through the back, and who later sneaks back on again the same way.*

COWPOKE 88: Seems as how we oughta have *somethin* fer the Kid tuh shoot at, though!

COWPOKE 89: Seems like it!

COWPOKE 90: Hey, how bout them Injuns over by Doc's place?

COWPOKE 91: That's thinkin, podnuh!

COWPOKE 92: Let's git the Kid some Injuns!

COWPOKE 93: (*shouting out through the swinging doors toward the men who have been dragging "the Marshall" out*) Hey, Clem! Go brang us some Injuns fer the Kid tuh shoot!

> *At the first two occasions of the word "Injun,"* THE KID *has spun, and now with the third he fires wildly toward the swinging doors. All* COWPOKES *within range drop to the floor, covering their heads, or dive under tables.*

COWPOKE 94: Whoa there, podnuh!

COWPOKE 95: Look out!

COWPOKE 96: Boy, jist say the word "Injun" and—!

> THE KID *again spins and fires, and this* COWPOKE *dives for cover. For the first time,* THE KID *seems to have lost control. He is suddenly jittery, wild, impulsive. In the lines that follow, the* COWPOKES *are actually playing with* THE KID *like a trapped animal, alternating the lines from one side of the set to the*

other, keeping THE KID *spinning.* THE KID *blasts away at every mention of "Injuns," but for all the wild shooting, none of the* COWPOKES *is hit. The* BELLES *stay out of this game, but may scurry out from behind one table to another, pop up like a jack-in-the-box from behind the bar, etc.*

COWPOKE 97: Whoopee! It's shore plain he don't like Injuns—! (*Blam!*)

COWPOKE 98: *No* kindsa Injuns! (*Blam!*)

COWPOKE 99: Nuthin could be plainer than the Kid's policy on Injuns—! (*Blam!*)

COWPOKE 100: Seems like Injuns (*Blam!*) make the Kid see red, man! (*Blam! Blam!*)

COWPOKE 101: Haw haw! That's a good un! Yuh git it, Kid?

COWPOKE 102: Injuns (*Blam!*) makes the Kid see red! (*Blam!*)

COWPOKE 103: —Man! (*Blam!*)

COWPOKE 104: Haw haw! Looks kinder like even red (*Blam!*) makes the Kid see red, man! (*Blam! Blam!*)

COWPOKE 93: (*the one who first shouted for Indians*) Hey, Clem! Fergit them Injuns! (*Blam!*) We don't need em! (*Blam! Blam!*)

COWPOKE 105: We got all the damn Injuns (*Blam!*) we need right here without usin up real ones!

DEPUTY: (*bumbling in through the swinging doors*) Hey, fellas! Have yuh seen the Sheriff? I cain't—

COWPOKE 106: (*pointing at* THE DEPUTY) Hey, Kid! *There's* a Injun!

> THE KID *opens fire, both barrels blazing, and* THE DEPUTY *does a fancy dance, then scrambles for cover. While ducking:*

DEPUTY: I jist only come tuh ask yuh if (*Blam!*) the Sheriff (*Blam! Blam!*)—YOUCH!—if the Sheriff (*Blam! Blam!*)—Halp!—if he's been by (*Blam!*)—YOWEE! Escuse me, fellas! (*He hightails it out of there.*)

COWPOKE 107: Haw haw haw! Way tuh go, Kid!

COWPOKE 108: Hey, Kid! Behind the bar! More Injuns!

> THE KID *spins and blasts away.* THE BARKEEP *diving for cover. Amplified splintering noises again.*

COWPOKE 109: Look out, Kid! Comin in the doors!

> THE KID *wheels and blasts away at the swinging doors. They should leap and waggle on their hinges with the impact of the shots.*

COWPOKE 110: Down from the ceilin, Kid!

COWPOKE 111: Under the tables, Kid!

COWPOKE 112: Outa the walls, Kid!

COWPOKE 113: Under the chairs! Injuns!

THE KID *has been whirling, spinning, firing insanely in all directions. Suddenly, he runs out of ammunition. He pauses, breathing heavily. He seems confused, rattled. Slowly then, he gathers his wits, regains his former cool, and begins to reload his six-shooters. The* COWPOKES *and* BELLES, *meanwhile, get back on their feet, come out of the corners, brush themselves off, straighten their hats, etc.*

COWPOKE 114: Whoopee!

COWPOKE 115: Holy shit! He's somethin *else!*

COWPOKE 116: He's the best damn Kid I ever seen!

One of the BELLES *now sidles up behind* THE KID, *wraps her arms around him, strokes his chest.* THE KID *ignores her, busy with his pistols.*

BELLE 31: Now, how bout punchin a few holes in lil ole Belle, cowboy? (*No response.*) I mean, I ain't been shot up like that in a coon's age! (*No response. More desperately:*) I may not *look* Injun, Kid honey, but I'm all Injun down *here!* (*Strokes herself.* THE KID *stares at her coldly, then turns away. She withdraws, looking hurt.*)

COWPOKE 117: Belle hon, yuh better be thankful he ain't takin yuh on!

COWPOKE 118: Yuh know the legend, Belle!

COWPOKE 119: They say he don't carry the usual equipment down there!

COWPOKE 120: They say he's the only three-gun killer in the West, Belle!

COWPOKE 121: They say any lady sleeps with the Kid, Belle, she sleeps fer a good long spell!

BELLE 32: (*stepping forward*) Well, I heard that legend, boys, and it's nearly true. I'm a eye-witness and a little bit more!

COWPOKE 122: Tell us about it, Belle!

> BELLE *32 steps forward and sings "The Kid with Blue Eyes." Some* COWPOKES *perhaps accompany her on instruments as before, and interject "Yahoo's" and the like from time to time. They all sing the choral lines.* THE KID *remains generally aloof, though he seems at times, especially when his skills or appurtenances are being described, to be listening critically, making sure the song is accurate, showing disdain when the descriptions seem to him short of the mark. If desired,* BELLE *32 may use a hand microphone, amplified accompaniment.*

THE KID WITH BLUE EYES

Now, boys, yuh all know me, I was once purty wild,
I'd never been rode, I was easily riled!
I'd left many a cowpuncher lame or half dead
From tryin tuh break me and take me tuh bed!
They wasn't a cowboy in the whole bléssed West
That could stay in the saddle, I'd busted the best!
But, boys, lemme tell yuh, I got quite a surprise
The day I got bestrid by the Kid with Blue Eyes!

CHO: When she got bestrid by the Kid with Blue Eyes!

He was tall as a jackpine and mean as a skunk!
A blond blue-eyed beauty with plennya spunk!
He trampled the vineyards and made the earth quake!
As soon as I seen him I started tuh shake!
His hands was like lightnin, he roared when he spoke!
They wasn't a fuzztail that he hadn't broke!
They was ice in his heart and fire in his glance,
And he caused a tornado when he lowered his pants!

CHO: He stirred a tornado when he dropped his pants!

Well, his legs was like pillars, his cheeks was snow white!
His balls weighed a ton and packed real dynamite!
The rest yuh kin guess, but they's one thing tuh tell:
His weapon is big, but it's blacker than hell!
Yes, blacker than hell, you boys heard me right!
When I seen it it give me a turrible fright!
And they's another thing more, I'm tellin yuh true!
It is blacker than death and its eye is true blue!

CHO: Wow! blacker than death and an eye that's true blue!

Well, he leaps in the saddle and screws me down tight,
And he crawls to muh middle, but I goes on the fight;
I rears and I bucks and I goes up on high,
Take a gyratin jump, I'm feeling right spry!
I goes tuh sun-fishin, I'm shore feelin grand!
He'll have tuh be good before *my* ass he'll brand!
I rolls round on my side and I'm high in the skies—
But I still ain't unsaddled that Kid with Blue Eyes!

CHO: She still ain't got rid a that Kid with Blue Eyes!

Well, I make one last try tuh git outa his grip,
And I take the high dive, but he's clear got me whipped!

Then we hit with a jar that shore gives me a scare,
And I'm way down below him, I don't know jist where!
I'm all busted up and I'm sore and I'm lame!
That blond buckaroo is awinnin the game!
I feel like a million years older that day
When the Kid with Blue Eyes starts blastin away!

CHO: Oh, that Kid with Blue Eyes, he's ablastin away!

Now, I've told yuh it's black with a little blue eye,
But it's worse than that, boys, and I'll tell yuh why:
It's also as cold as the stone on a tomb
On a dead winter's night and it froze up muh womb!
So, boys, here's the moral tuh my little story:
They's all kindsa fame and they's all kindsa glory,
But as fer my own, I tell yuh no lies:
I wisht I'd never been rode by the Kid with Blue Eyes!

CHO: Oh yeah, she's been had by that Kid with Blue Eyes!

> *Loud applause and hallooing as the song ends.* THE
> KID *steps forward, and a hush falls.*

THE KID: (*flatly, as before*) Youpy youpy.

COWPOKE 123: Oh, hell yes, Kid! Ti yi youpy yea!

> *Again the gleeful chorus of "youpy yea's," inter-*
> *rupted as* THE SHERIFF *steps through the swinging*
> *doors. A sudden hush descends.* THE KID'S *back is to*
> *the doors, but he is taut, alert.* THE DEPUTY *creeps*
> *in abjectly on hands and knees, and hides behind*
> *the nearest available object.*

SHERIFF: You're at the end a yore rope, Kid.

Prolonged pause.

SHERIFF: I've . . . I've come tuh take yuh in.

Again a pause, all tense.

COWPOKE 124: (*softly, cautiously, as though trying to get* THE SHERIFF *to cool it*) Uh . . . Sheriff . . . *pssst!*

SHERIFF: (*shaking off the* COWPOKE *with a quick impatient gesture*) I'm askin yuh tuh go quiet, Kid . . .

> THE KID *suddenly whirls and draws.* THE SHERIFF *draws simultaneously, and there's an explosive exchange of gunfire.* THE SHERIFF, *almost disbelievingly, remains standing, as* THE KID, *surprised at his own wound, slowly crumples. Prolonged shocked silence, as* THE KID *sinks to the floor and dies. The whole saloon is momentarily spellbound.* THE SHERIFF *breaks it giddily.*

SHERIFF: Hey! I'll be durned! Hey, I—I *done* it! I got him, boys! *I got the Kid!*

> COWPOKES *stare at* THE SHERIFF *with astonishment, disappointment, even some gathering disgust. Silence maintains until* COWPOKE *125 steps forward, looks down at* THE KID, *then up at* THE SHERIFF.

COWPOKE 125: (*genuinely upset*) Aw shucks, Sheriff! Yuh fucked it up!

DEPUTY: (*creeping out from hiding*) What'd he do?

COWPOKE 125: (*again*) Hell, he killt the goddamn Kid!

DEPUTY: (*standing now, moving forward to see for himself, no longer the comic foil*) Oh, *shit!*

COWPOKE 126: Christ, whadda we do *now?*

COWPOKE 127: (*disbelievingly*) He jist gunned him down!

SHERIFF: (*confused by this reception, but still smiling, still a little delirious over his unexpected victory*) I . . . I don't git it, fellas! What's the matter . . . ?

> *A brief moment of general indecision and frustration, while* THE SHERIFF *speaks, the* COWPOKES *and* BELLES *looking at each other for ways of getting on with it,* THE DEPUTY *gazing thoughtfully at* THE SHERIFF. *Then,* THE DEPUTY, *who has emerged suddenly as the authority present, calls the* COWPOKES *nearest him into a huddle—and they swing almost immediately into a sudden celebrative mood, led by the three* COWPOKES *who complained above.* THE DEPUTY's *word is quickly passed to the other* COWPOKES *and* BELLES.

DEPUTY: (*back in weak-kneed comic character*) Good golly! Wha—what happened?

COWPOKE 125: (*again*) Hey! The Sheriff got him!

COWPOKE 126: (*again*) What!!!

COWPOKE 127: (*again*) He got the Kid! The Kid is dead!

DEPUTY: Jumpin gee-willikers!

THE SHERIFF *is having trouble following all this, but he gradually gives in to the flattery, stops trying to puzzle it out.*

COWPOKE 128: He outshot the Kid!

COWPOKE 129: They said it couldn't be done!

COWPOKE 130: But the Sheriff done it!

DEPUTY: Waal, I'll be horn-swoggled!

COWPOKE 131: He's gotta be *it*, boys!

COWPOKE 132: *The fastest gun in the West!*

BELLE 33: *The fastest gun in the West!*

COWPOKE 133: *The fastest goddamn gun in the West!*

SHERIFF: (*chuckling awkwardly in genuine embarrassment, still somewhat confused*) Now . . . now, fellas . . .

COWPOKE 134: Hey! Let's set em up fer the Sheriff!

COWPOKE 135: Hey, bartender!

COWPOKE 136: Hey, consarn it! Git a leg on! This calls fer a goddamn celybration!

THE BARKEEP *hurries back behind the bar, lines up shotglasses on the bar, pours out drinks. He is kept hustling throughout the scene that follows, as* COW-POKES *and* BELLES *contrive to get* THE SHERIFF *thoroughly drunk.*

COWPOKE 137: To the fastest gun!

They cheer, drink, pour out more.

COWPOKE 138: The Sheriff has saved our goddamn town, boys!

SHERIFF: (*holding back*) Lissen, boys, I . . .

BELLE 34: He's made it safe tuh walk in the streets agin!

COWPOKE 139: He's saved the West!

BELLE 35: He's number one!

COWPOKE 140: He shot the Kid!

SHERIFF: Well, now, yuh don't understand. It wasn't nuthin . . .

COWPOKE 141: That's right, Sheriff! It wasn't nuthin! Nuthin but the greatest thing that's ever happened tuh the whole goddamn West!

BELLE 36: The Sheriff's done made *histry*, boys!

COWPOKE 142: Drink up, Sheriff! Drink up, boys!

COWPOKE 143: Tuh histry!

COWPOKE 144: Tuh the West!

COWPOKE 145: Tuh the fastest gun!

BELLE 37: (*seductively, as all the* BELLES *work at getting* THE SHERIFF *loaded*) You kin make *my* lil ole histry *any* time, Sheriff hon!

COWPOKE 146: Whew! Jist lookit that coyote lyin there dead!

COWPOKE 147: All shot tuh shit, man!

Throughout this scene, THE DEPUTY, *while hopping about giddily, sloshing drinks around, etc., is at the same time passing instructions, whipping up the frenzy, maybe even providing the speakers with their lines. Now he stops midstage and declaims drunkenly:*

DEPUTY: Crime don't pay, boys!

COWPOKE 148: Haw haw! Yer durn tootin, it don't!

COWPOKE 149: Haw haw! The Kid here kin tell yuh, pod-nuh!

COWPOKE 150: Shit, the Kid cain't tell yuh *nuthin,* man!

COWPOKE 151: Haw haw!

SHERIFF: (*pleased with himself, but sill wanting to make some point or other*) Right! That's right! About crime, I mean! It don't pay! And not only that—!

COWPOKE 152: (*cutting him off*) That's right, ain't it, boys? It don't!

COWPOKE 153: Not when yuh got the number one gun in the West fer Sheriff!

COWPOKE 154: Haw haw! That's tellin it, podnuh!

COWPOKE 155: Consarn it, boys, let's hear it fer the Sheriff!

ALL: (*loudly, arms raised in a toast*) YOUPY TI YI
YOUPY YOUPY YEA!

> THE SHERIFF *tries, without effect, to protest; then
> uneasily drinks with the others. A* BELLE, *seeing his
> reluctance, tips the glass up for him (in pretended
> flirtation) to make sure he drinks it all. He stands
> away from the bar.*

SHERIFF: (*with feeling*) Thank yuh, boys. Thank yuh. It's
right kind of yuh, I mean that. But . . . uh . . . mebbe
this ain't exackly the best time tuh—

COWPOKE 156: Ain't the best time, Sheriff? After all that's
happened?

COWPOKE 157: Tuh celybrate the conquest a *evil*, Sheriff?

COWPOKE 158: Why, Sheriff! This is gonna be a national
holiday!

SHERIFF: (*embarrassed, not convinced, but flattered, turning to look down at his victim*) Well, mebbe, but I was
thinkin mebbe first we oughta bury the Kid here . . .

COWPOKE 159: Say a few prayers, Sheriff? Is that it? Say a
few prayers over the Kid?

COWPOKE 160: Prayers! Haw haw! The Sheriff wants tuh say
a prayer, boys!

COWPOKE 161: Let's have a prayer, boys! A prayer fer the
Kid!

The COWPOKES *remove their hats, assume woeful ex-
pressions, put their heads together, and joined by the*
BELLES, *commence to sing a kind of dirge or plain-
chant:*

ALL: YOUPY YOUPY COMA TI YI YOUPY—

THE SHERIFF *looks a little troubled.* THE DEPUTY
notices this.

DEPUTY: *(interrupting sternly)* Now, wait a minute, boys!
Wait jist a dadblame minute here! I won't have yuh
makin riddycule a the efFICKacy a prayer! Why, many's
the time when the Sheriff and me, we seen prayer come
through when nuthin else'd work! Ain't it so, Sheriff?
Why, remember Ash Holler! And Bad Axe! Sand
Crick! Mountain Meaders!

The COWPOKES *and* BELLES *look abashed, drift apart,
as before.*

DEPUTY: And, Zeb, you was there when we had tuh massa-
cree them Pueblos, what would we a done that day, ifn
it hadn'ta been fer prayer?

Someone acknowledges this for "Zeb."

DEPUTY: Why, it was like that time along the Snake River
back in '49! Remember that time, Sheriff?

THE SHERIFF *doesn't look like he remembers. Somebody has filled his glass again. He drinks absently.*

COWPOKE 162: Along the Snake? Hey, ain't that the time them Injuns whupped up a thunderstorm or somethin, Deppity?

DEPUTY: Yup, but that weren't the end of it!

COWPOKE 163: Weren't the end of it!

COWPOKE 164: Yuh mean, it was wuss'n that, Deppity?

DEPUTY: It was wuss'n that, boys . . . and it was better!

COWPOKE 165: Huh! Sounds like the beginnins of a story, Deppity!

> *The* COWPOKES *settle back to hear a story,* THE SHERIFF *among them. Throughout the story, the* BELLES *and* COWPOKES *work at their project of getting* THE SHERIFF *drunk, the* COWPOKES *slipping over one by one to have a toast with him, the* BELLES *cuddling him and tipping drinks down him playfully, etc.* THE DEPUTY *commences the tale in his natural voice, then fades out as amplified (radio) sounds and voices—indicated by (V) in the script below—fade in. Preferably, sounds and voices should be broadcast stereophonically from amplifiers situated all around the auditorium. During the amplified portions,* THE DEPUTY *engages in a pantomime, not so much of the different speaking parts, as of basic emotions and gestures (fear, effort, victory, confusion, self-defense, etc.).* THE DEPUTY *can work out his own set of movements pursuant to his vision of the material, using barroom gear, the dead*

body of THE KID, *the* COWPOKES *and* BELLES, *as he
wishes. If he designates a* COWPOKE *to "play"* THE
SHERIFF *at any point, he may "borrow"* THE
SHERIFF'*s star and pin it on the* COWPOKE, *where
it remains to the end of the play.* THE DEPUTY'*s performance should suggest priestly rituals, the magic
gestures with validity of their own, prior to the
"story" being amplified over them. Emphasis in the
latter should be on sound effects, voice tones, and
the implications of actions (the words themselves
can well be lost at times).* BELLES *and* COWPOKES
*may form shifting choral groups that respond antiph-
onally to the turns of the story.*

DEPUTY: Well, yes, boys, so it is, and it happened like this.
Me and the Sheriff had signed on as outriders with a
wagon train fulla prospectors headin out west to civilize
Utah, and we hadn't no more'n reached the Sangre de
Cristo Pass, when suddenly we got set upon by a buncha
wild Injuns, Lord, they was comin at us . . . (*fade out as
radio voices and the noise of wagons rolling and squeaking, horses clip-clipping, shouts, etc., fade in* . . .)

DEPUTY(V): (*shouting in panic*) . . . Lord, they're comin at
us from all four directions, Sheriff! Comanches! And
Navahos, too! We're done for!

*Simultaneously: distant galloping and wahooing of
attacking Indians. Horses nearby whinny with fear.
General confusion in the wagon train.*

SHERIFF (V): (*shouting over the panic*) Stop blubberin, podnuh, and draw a bead! Quick, you men! Git them wagons pulled around there! C'mon, boys! Pluck up! Git a leg on! Tip em over there!

> *Crash of wagons being wheeled around, tipped over. Confused shouts. Galloping and wahooing augments. Rifle shots and ricocheting bullets. Thuds of arrows striking wood. Occasional screams and grunts as Indians bite the dust or settlers fall wounded. Meanwhile:*

SETTLER (V): We ain't got a chance, Sheriff!

SETTLER (V): They come up on us too fast!

SETTLER (V): Look out! Comin up behind! It's—*AAR-RGHH!*

SETTLER (V): It's Apaches! They're gangin up on us!

DEPUTY (V): Goldurn it, Sheriff! It ain't fair!

SHERIFF (V): C'mon, don't give it up, boys! While they's still one of us alive and kickin, they ain't won the day!

SETTLER (V): It's no use, Sheriff!

SETTLER (V): We'll never hold out!

SETTLER (V): Hey! What's that I hear, boys?

DEPUTY (V): (*blubbering*) Ain't nuthin out thar but mad crazy red varmints, and they—

SHERIFF (V): No, wait, Deppity! Lissen! I hear it, too!

*Distantly, behind the Indian whooping and holler-
ing: the bugle call of the U.S. Cavalry, the crack of
rifle fire.*

DEPUTY(V): Durn muh britches! it's the Cavalry! boys, it's
the Cavalry!

*Shouts of joy as Cavalry noises augment. The Indi-
ans fall into confusion. The settlers shout encour-
agement, as the Cavalry put the Indians to rout. Indian noises diminish and disappear. Horses gallop
up, snort and whinny, as settlers cheer, proclaim
victory, etc.*

DEPUTY(V): Hey, you fellers come jist in time!

COLONEL(V): Howdy, Deppity! Howdy, Sheriff!

SHERIFF(V): Howdy, Colonel! Say, it shore was great to
hear you boys comin over the hill! We was in a bad
state—

COLONEL(V): Well, Sheriff, yuh ain't outa hot water yet!
Scouts tell us they's tribes a Pawnee and Walapai up
ahead, and when these Comanches who got away have
joined em—say, did yuh see who was ridin with them
Comanches?

SETTLER(V): Navahos, Colonel!

SETTLER(V): And Apaches!

SHERIFF(V): Mebbe some Flatheads, too, though it was
hard tuh see fer sure.

DEPUTY(V): Ain't none of em got heads yuh'd call normal!

Off-mike laughter.

SHERIFF(V): Whadda yuh think we oughta do, Colonel?

COLONEL(V): Well, Sheriff, I reckon yuh better keep the wagons movin, git out from under these bluffs before sundown!

SETTLER(V): Ain't yuh comin along with us, Colonel?

COLONEL(V): Yuh got the Sheriff and his Deppity here tuh help, we'll move on ahead, see what we kin do about mebbe clearin the way fer yuh a mite.

SHERIFF(V): Thanks, Colonel! Thanks a lot!

The settlers echo THE SHERIFF'*s sentiments. Fade out.*

Fade in: sounds of the wagon train rumbling along. A horse gallops up.

SETTLER(V): (*shouting as he approaches*) Hey, Sheriff! It's gonna be dark purty quick! Reckon we oughta pull up now, or—?

SHERIFF(V): I dunno! Seems tuh me as how we mebbe oughta wait fer the Colonel tuh—hold on! There they come now!

Sounds of Cavalry galloping up.

COLONEL(V): (*off mike*) Whoa, there!

Horse whinnies and snorts. Sounds of greetings.

SHERIFF (V): Hullo, Colonel! How's it look up thar?

COLONEL(V): Bad, Sheriff! We wiped out the Walapai okay, but they's still the Pawnee and the others, and they's signs a Cheyenne and Blackfeet comin tuh join em, they got a real united pow-wow goin! And . . . somethin *wuss'n* that!

DEPUTY(V): What? Wha—what's happenin up thar, Colonel?

COLONEL(V): (*gravely*) They've started up a rain dance!

Settlers gasp and mutter.

SETTLER(V): Mebbe it's time fer us tuh do a little prayin of our own, boys!

Sounds of approval and general anxiety.

SETTLER(V): (*off mike*) We could pray fer the measles or the smallpox tuh come down on em! We've worked that lotsa places!

SHERIFF (V): No, I don't think we wanna bother gittin God in on it yet, men! He's done a whole heap fer us already, what with the Colt and these new breech-loadin rifles, I think it's up tuh us tuh stand on our own two feet! Leastways, long as we kin! Whadda *you* think, Colonel?

COLONEL(V): That's right, Sheriff! We ain't run clean outa our own resources yet! Ain't I seen some dynamite in some a these wagons?

SETTLER(V): Yeah, we're fixin tuh take that tuh Virginia City, Colonel, tuh git at that silver!

COLONEL(V): Yup, well, we won't need but a coupla bundles or so. And somebody tuh trap two or three buzzards.

SETTLER(V): Buzzards!

DEPUTY(V): Whoa, Colonel! You ain't been eatin some a them Injun mushrooms, have yuh?

There is a distant rumble of thunder.

COLONEL(V): Yuh heard me! And on the double, boys! That was thunder! We ain't got much time!

General shouts of settlers rushing off to get dynamite and buzzards, widespread anxiety. More thundering.

SHERIFF(V): Hey, I git it, Colonel! Yuh reckon tuh upset that prayer-meetin a theirs a mite!

COLONEL(V): That's right, Sheriff. The buzzard, as yuh know, is the Injuns' thunder bird. They figger it avenges em agin their enemies, and part a ever rain dance cerymony is when they attract these buzzards down and smear em with the blood a white men. Only, huh! this time them Injuns is gonna git a little lesson in the futility and foolishness a their heathen superstitions! (*Fade out.*)

Fade in: sounds of thunder, high winds, light rain.

COLONEL(V): (*shouting over storm*) All right, shake a leg, men! Yuh got the dynamite tied tuh them buzzards?

Sounds of birds flapping and squawking, shouts of "Yup! ready tuh go!" etc., amid the storm.

COLONEL(V): All right! Let em go!

Sounds of flapping wings, squawks and mews, disappearing into the gathering storm.

SETTLER(V): It's startin to blow purty turrible, Colonel! Ifn this don't work . . .

COLONEL(V): It'll work. What we gotta hope is it works fast enough!

Storm sounds augment. Horses whinny and people shout, trying to hold things down, etc.

SETTLER(V): (*shouting desperately over the storm*) We ain't gonna make it, Colonel!

SETTLER(V): (*ditto*) It's too late!

SETTLER(V): (*ditto*) Hurricane!

COLONEL(V): (*shouting over the storm and panic, sound of his horse rearing about, whinnying*) Hang fast there, you jaspers!

SHERIFF(V): (*ditto*) Git a grip, men! Deppity, git over thar and help that family hold down their gear!

COLONEL(V): (*ditto*) Any man lose his head, I'm puttin a bullet through it! What'd yuh come West fer? Did yuh

think it was some kinda tea party out here? C'mon, git
the lead outa yore britches!

> *Sudden distant but terrific explosion. Storm sounds*
> *diminish. Men cheer and whistle: "Whoopee! We*
> *done it!" etc.*

SHERIFF(V): (*a little breathless from exertion*) Whew!
gotta hand it to yuh, Colonel! That one was a stroke a
genius!

DEPUTY(V): (*ditto*) Whoo-ee! I ain't felt so good since ole
Custer went one way and we went t'other!

COLONEL(V): Yup, well, we may not be in the clear yet!
Them damn heathens may not dance em up another rain
fer a spell, but we probably ain't seen the last of em!

SETTLER(V): (*off mike*) All right, men, it's gittin dark! Let's
make camp here tonight! (*Campmaking noises, horse*
whinnies, etc.) We got a long day ahead of us!

COLONEL(V): (*private to* THE SHERIFF) And I hope we
see it, Sheriff! I hope we see it! (*Fade out.*)

COWPOKE 166: Wow! That was some story, Deppity!

COWPOKE 167: Wasn't that buzzard trick somethin, though?

COWPOKE 168: Like the Sheriff said, a—what'd you say,
Sheriff?

> THE SHERIFF *looks up blearily, half-smiling. Some-*
> *body pours him a drink. The* COWPOKES *shift*

about a bit in this interval, pouring fresh drinks, attending to THE SHERIFF, *pinching* BELLE *bottoms, etc.* THE DEPUTY, *who has paused in his mime, now scrutinizes* THE SHERIFF *briefly.*

COWPOKE 169: A stroke a genius! That's what the Sheriff said!

COWPOKE 170: Right, too! Stroke a genius!

COWPOKE 171: I bet all yuh could see a them Injuns after that was their hairy red hunkers ahumpin acrost the hills like ninety!

General laughter.

DEPUTY: No, boys, that's where you're wrong!

COWPOKE 172: (*disbelievingly*) What! Yuh mean them dumb Injuns hadn't learnt their lesson yet?

DEPUTY: That's right. In fact, they durn near put us all under sod that night! I tell yuh, it was a bad un! One oldtimer even tried tuh make out as how it was the Colonel's fault, usin firepower like that agin the Injun gods, said it was a sacrilege, and even the God of our own fathers mightn't look on it too kindly!

COWPOKE 173: Huh! Somebody shoulda shot that oldtimer!

General laughter and approval.

DEPUTY: Now, boys, yuh know that ain't our way! Ever man's got a right tuh his own way a thinkin!

COWPOKE 174: Yeah, and he's got a right tuh git shot fer it, too!

Laughter and approval.

COWPOKE 175: But what happened, Deppity?

DEPUTY: Well, I was jist inta my third plate a jerk and beans and a sweet widder, when this scoutin party come back and says more Injuns has gathered, Chippewas, Arapaho, and Nez Perce among em now, and they was up tuh some peculiar religious cerymony, the likes a which they ain't never seen before! That was when this oldtimer spoke up, gripin bout that buzzard flimflam, and makin out as how the white man didn't stand a chance agin the Injun . . . *(fade out)*

OLDTIMER(V): *(fade in over* DEPUTY'S *words)* . . . agin the Injun on his own huntin ground. Oh, it was different when we was fightin em back East, we wasn't all alone back there, we could always skedaddle back and git more guns and grub and help, ifn we needed to, and what we did, we did on accounta we had to, on accounta we was supposed to! But we wasn't supposed tuh cross the ole Miss, no, we been pushin God's hand—

SETTLER(V): Aw, oldtimer, you're always bitchin! A few years ago, you was skeered tuh cross the Appalachias!

OLDTIMER(V): Now you lissen, I'm tellin yuh fer yer own good! Out here, the Injuns is gonna whup us! They know the land, they kin come out of it from nowhere and disappear right into it again, you see how they do it! They're fightin fer their homes and we—

SETTLER(V): Yeah, but they're *heathens*, oldtimer! They ain't much better'n animals, they're jist game meant fer shootin, and ifn we cain't—

OLDTIMER(V): That's jist it! Animals! They got a feelin fer this land, and we ain't! We cain't do nuthin but blow it up—

COLONEL(V): (*galloping up*) What's all this bullroarin about, oldtimer?

DEPUTY(V): All these spooky Injun cerymonies tonight has got the old feller shook up, Colonel. He thinks them dumb nekkid savages has got a chance agin us Christian gentlemen!

   General laughter.

OLDTIMER(V): (*irate*) All right! You jist keep alaughin! But you'll see which side a yore mouth you're laughin outa tomorry! Ifn yuh still got one and we ain't all been scalped—!

SHERIFF(V): (*interrupting*) Now, take it easy, oldtimer! It's a long haul, it ain't easy, I admit, but we *know* more'n they do, and we always will and sooner or later—

OLDTIMER(V): But I'm tellin yuh, Sheriff, the kindsa things we know ain't never gonna do us no good out here! This ain't Virginny! It ain't even Illinois! We're jist gittin ourselves killt fer nuthin!

SETTLER(V): Gold ain't nuthin, oldtimer!

SETTLER(V): Land ain't nuthin! Furs and silver ain't nuthin!

SHERIFF(V): But, Colonel, what's all this about peculiar cerymonies?

COLONEL(V): I dunno exackly, Sheriff. Mebbe they're jist stallin fer time. Anyhow, I don't think tonight we're apt tuh—

Distant rumbling noise.

DEPUTY(V): Woops! What's that rumblin noise?

COLONEL(V): I dunno!

OLDTIMER(V): Yuh dunno, Colonel? Well, I ain't surprised! It's like I'm tellin yuh, you're never gonna hold this land agin the Injuns! I kin tell yuh what that is! It's bad news, that's what it is!

Rumbling augments. Anxiety again starts to sweep the wagon train.

SETTLER(V): (*anxiously*) What is it, oldtimer? What is it?

OLDTIMER(V): That's a herd a buffalo, son! Mebbe lotsa herds all at once! They're stampedin! And they're headin this way!

SETTLER(V): Here comes a scout!

SCOUT(V): (*galloping up*) Colonel! Colonel! They're comin at us from all round us!

COLONEL(V): (*alarmed*) What's comin?

SCOUT(V): (*breathless*) Buffalo. Elk. Wild horses. Longhorns. Even grizzlies and wolves! It's the damnedest thing yuh ever seen!

Rumbling steadily augments.

OLDTIMER(V): What'd I tell yuh, boys!

COLONEL(V): Shut up, oldtimer! Everbody git hitched up! Quick! We may have tuh move outa here fast! C'mon!

SHERIFF(V): I'll ride out and see what I kin see, Colonel!

He gallops off. Rumbling augments. Shouts of confusion and nighttime terror amid the preparations. Wild whinnies and shouts of struggle.

SETTLER(V): Colonel! All the horses is goin wild! We cain't control em!

SETTLER(V): Our cattle is breakin loose! It's like they gone crazy!

SETTLER(V): One of our dogs is eatin my baby!

DEPUTY(V): Whadda we gonna *do*, Colonel?

COLONEL(V): I dunno! Them goddamn Injuns! But we gotta think a somethin, Deppity, and damn quick! Lissen! Do yuh hear warwhoops?

Amid the augmenting rumble of the advancing herds: the distant warwhoops of thousands of Indians.

DEPUTY(V): Here comes the Sheriff back, Colonel!

SHERIFF (V): (*galloping up*) Injuns, Colonel! Millions of em! Follerin up the herds! It's like as how each tribe is comin with its own kinda beast!

COLONEL(V): My God! So that's it!

SHERIFF (V): I reckon the time's come, Colonel. I reckon it's time tuh pray.

> *Rumbling, panic augmenting.*

COLONEL(V): I hate tuh admit it, Sheriff. But I think you're right! (*Shouting:*) All right, men! Everbody on his knees! Is there a preacher among us?

SETTLER(V): (*shouting from near distance*) The oldtimer's done some preachin, Colonel!

> *Rumbling and warwhooping, whinnying and general turmoil, all rapidly augmenting.*

COLONEL(V): All right, they're nearly on us! C'mon, oldtimer! Let's git tuh singin! let's git tuh prayin!

OLDTIMER(V): (*shouting above the turmoil with evangelical fervor*) Remember the Book, boys! Remember what it says! It says, And the Lord said, I have surely seen the affliction a my people!

ALL(V): Yes, Lord! Hear us!

OLDTIMER(V): And he says, I know their sorrows!

ALL(V): Oh, God of our fathers, help us! Help us in our sorrows! Help us in our time a need!

OLDTIMER(V): And he says, I am come down tuh deliver em outa this here land, and I'm gonna brang em up unto a good land!

ALL(V): Yes, Lord, save us, Lord!

OLDTIMER(V): Yes, a good land, and a large land! Yes, he says, I'm gonna deliver you unto a land flowin with milk and honey! Do yuh hear me, boys! Flowin with milk and honey!

ALL(V): Milk and honey, Lord! Oh, they're comin, Lord! Hurry, Lord! Hurry!

Herds and Indians thundering down on them. They shout above the deafening noise.

OLDTIMER(V): And he says, I'm gonna stretch out muh hand and smite yore enemies with all muh wonders, says he! Go git the elders and let em see!

ALL(V): Oh yeah, God! Smite em, God! Hurry, God! Save us!

OLDTIMER(V): And I'm gonna give this people favor—!

COLONEL(V): (*shouting above the rest*) Wait! What's that?

Distantly, behind the thunder of hooves and howls and whinnies: a train whistle.

DEPUTY(V): I dunno, Colonel! But ifn I was back East, I'd say that was—

SHERIFF(V): It is, Deppity! It is! Look, Colonel, there tuh the East! It's a train! It's comin outa nowhere!

> *Train blowin loud and clear now, but still at some distance. Slowly it augments until its thunder matches the thunder of the stampede. The settlers sing "The Battle Hymn of the Republic."*

SETTLER(V): Lookit that light! *It's bearin down on us!*

DEPUTY(V): *We're all gonna git killt!*

OLDTIMER(V): (*still shouting, his voice fading in over the tumult, then out again*) . . . and he says, you shalt take water outa the river and pour it on the dry land, and that there water, took outa the river, it shall become blood on the dry land! Yes, and it shall come tuh pass . . .

SETTLER(V): (*shouting over the tumult, praying, etc.*) They're breakin! The herds is breakin!

SETTLER(V): (*ditto*) Lookit em there in the light! They're turnin tail!

> *Train roar now much louder than the stampede. Sounds of frantic whooping, screaming, whinnying, etc. Train roars by, then slowly fades. As it fades, it is the only sound heard, except for a few settlers still singing strands of "The Battle Hymn of the Republic," Fade out.*

THE DEPUTY *fades in, in time with the voices fading out, singing "The Battle Hymn of the Republic" alone, squeakily, out of tune.*

COWPOKE 176: (*interrupting*) Wow! Yuh mean that a train jist come outa nowhere like that, and sent all them Injuns and buffalo ascatterin?!

DEPUTY: Yup, it come and went, jist like that, *whoosh!* roarin outa the East, fadin off inta the West, outa the night and inta the night, and when it had gone, they wasn't no sign a them Injuns nor all them herds they'd wizarded up like that! Weren't no rails nor tracks nor nuthin! And somethin else, boys: I seen it go by. It had "The Train a Peace" writ on it! And they weren't nobody drivin that train! *Nobody!*

COWPOKE 177: Whew! Right outa the night!

COWPOKE 178: And nobody up there!

COWPOKE 179: Makes yuh think, don't it!

COWPOKE 180: Makes yuh learn a little humility, don't it!

COWPOKE 181: Whew! That was some story, Deppity!

COWPOKE 182: Them were the days, boys! It was a great ole place then!

COWPOKE 183: That's when the West was the fuckin West!

COWPOKE 184: They had all the fun back then! (*Gazing down on* THE KID:) Now all we got left is . . .

He gives THE KID's *body an irritable boot.*

COWPOKE 185: How come you never told us about that, Sheriff?

> THE SHERIFF *is very drunk. He stands blearily away from the bar and* BELLES, *but cannot see too clearly who has spoken to him.*

SHERIFF: Well . . . uh . . . tuh tell the truth, I don't rightly—

DEPUTY: (*interrupting*) Hey, boys! We plumb fergot! I shouldn't be tellin all these here stories! This here's the Sheriff's day!

COWPOKE 186: (*with difficulty mustering enthusiasm*) Yeah, right, right. He killt the Kid, didn't he?

COWPOKE 187: (*picking it up*) That's it! Shot him down! Last damn Kid we'll ever git, too!

BELLE 38: He's our man!

COWPOKE 188: (*raising his glass*) Here's tuh the Sheriff, boys!

COWPOKE 189: Tuh the Sheriff!

ALL: YOUPY YOUPY TI YI—

SHERIFF: *Hold on, boys!*

> *He gestures with his hand, spilling some of his drink. Stares at it curiously, then drinks it off.*

SHERIFF: Boys . . . boys . . . thank yuh! But . . .

> *Again he gestures, and again he interrupts himself to stare at the glass. Working methodically, he pivots*

carefully, sets the glass firmly on the bar, nearly knocks it off trying to let go of it, then turns around, hands on his lapels, to face the BELLES *and* COWPOKES. *Trying to look wise, he raises one hand as though to ask for silence, though in fact no one is speaking.*

SHERIFF: Yuh ask . . . about the story . . . (*He belches.*)

COWPOKE 190: (*hastily interrupting*) Hold it, Sheriff! Belle here's got somethin tuh say tuh yuh! (*Hoarse urgent whisper:*) The six-shooters, Belle!

He shoves BELLE 39 *forward, as* THE BARKEEP *hurriedly refills* THE SHERIFF's *glass. One of the* COWPOKES *shoves the glass into* THE SHERIFF's *hand.*

BELLE 39: (*hurried and uncertain at first, but with increasing seductiveness*) Uh, Sheriff, seein as yuh . . . Sheriff, why, seein as how you're now the fastest gun in the West, seems like, seems tuh me like yuh oughta put . . . yuh oughta be wearin them fancy silver shootin irons, Sheriff . . . (*She casts a suggestive glance down at* THE KID.)

SHERIFF: (*still in a drunken declamatory stance*) Hunh? . . . Well . . . well, Belle, that's jist it, I was jist gonna . . . yuh mean the Kid's—? Aw . . . well, thanks, Belle . . . but I don't reckon—

COWPOKE 191: (*interrupting*) Hey! Yuh got a point there, Belle!

COWPOKE 192: The Kid's shootin irons!

COWPOKE 193: He earned em!

COWPOKE 194: Damn if he didn't!

SHERIFF: Aw, thanks, fellas . . . but, no, I—

COWPOKE 195: Sheriff, git that ugly old gunbelt off!

> *The* BELLES *and* COWPOKES *hastily strip a mildly protesting* SHERIFF *of his gunbelt, while others remove the belt from* THE KID's *body. They handle* THE KID's *weapons gingerly, as though carelessness might trigger them off. This is just the first step in the transformation of* THE SHERIFF *into a kind of makeshift ragtag* KID. *In what follows, the* BELLES *should take a major role in dressing* THE SHERIFF, *keeping him distracted with little caresses, kisses, etc. He mumbles in incoherent protest, the only person present, in fact, free to mutter or ad-lib conversationally. As the girls strip* THE KID, *they might occasionally look with undisguised longing on his body, maybe even get a quick kick in the rump from one of the* COWPOKES *for not moving fast enough.*

COWPOKE 196: And lookit them fancy white gloves! Our Sheriff should oughta have him a pair a gloves like them!

COWPOKE 197: And boots! Hombre! Them white boots is plumb outa sight!

COWPOKE 198: You said it, podnuh!

BELLE 40: Take a mighty big man tuh step inta *them* boots!

COWPOKE 199: And, Belle, we *got* the *man!*

DEPUTY: Boys, I ain't never seen a Stetson purty as this un! (*Puts* THE KID's *hat on his own head, and it falls down around his ears.*)

COWPOKE 200: (*grabbing* THE KID's *hat off* THE DEPUTY's *head angrily*) Whoa there! Whaddaya doin?

COWPOKE 201: Who do yuh think yuh are, cowboy?

COWPOKE 202: Did *you* outgun the Kid, podnuh?

DEPUTY: (*shamefacedly*) Well . . . uh . . . no, but—

COWPOKE 200: (*again*) Only one man in town got a right tuh *that* hat, hombre! And you ain't him! (*Clamps the hat grandly on* THE SHERIFF's *head.*)

COWPOKE 203: (*admiring* THE SHERIFF *in his new duds*) Hey now! Take a lookit *that*, boys!

COWPOKE 204: Hah! he's gittin there!

SHERIFF: Now, jist hold on one minute—!

BELLE 41: Jumpin gee-willikers, ain't he a pitcher!

COWPOKE 205: Here, lemme see him!

COWPOKE 206: No, turn him thisaway—hey now!

> *They spin him about, getting him dizzy and confused.*

COWPOKE 207: What about the pants and shirt?

COWPOKE 208: Yuh reckon he needs em?

SHERIFF: Now, doggone it, fellas—!

BELLE 42: Hey, boys, I seen some right purty critters in my day, but I ain't never seen nuthin tuh match this un!

BELLE 43: Ain't he somethin, though!

The BELLES caress him, turn him about, while the COWPOKES continue to strip THE KID. THE SHERIFF breaks free. He is flustered, excited, troubled, breathing irregularly.

SHERIFF: NOW, KNOCK IT OFF, I SAID!!

The COWPOKES, taken aback, leave THE KID lie, turn to attend THE SHERIFF, effective at last. He calms, but watches them warily. They are alert, intent, sober. THE SHERIFF is struggling to be clear-headed about it all, but is ultimately too befuddled.

SHERIFF: Okay. Okay. I know yuh mean well. I know. Appreciation. I understand. You're thinkin, what kin we do fer the Sheriff, after all . . . you know, after what he's done fer us. Killt the Kid and all. Hell, boys, I'd feel the same way, any decent man would.

COWPOKE 209: Aw, lissen, fergit it, Sheriff! Drink up!

They all press forward again, picking up in the game where they left off.

COWPOKE 210: Tuh the Sheriff, boys!

COWPOKE 211: Tuh the fastest—

SHERIFF: (*authoritatively*) NO, DAMMIT, HOLD ON! (*They stop short.*) I ain't said muh piece, boys! (*They shrug, glance impatiently at one another.*) So jist take a grip on yore feelins there and hear me out, cuz it's somethin yuh gotta know! (*He pauses, as though thinking it all out, swaying some, belching.*) What I wanted tuh say was this. Somethin like this. Well, okay. It was me or the Kid. That's easy tuh folla. And the Kid got it. But . . . but it coulda jist as easy been me, see? (*He pauses, frowning.*) No . . . no, that ain't it. That ain't exackly right. Whoo! Ifn I didn't know you boys better, I'd say yuh was tryin tuh git me drunk! (*He chuckles loosely, but laughs alone.*) See, what I'm tryin tuh tell yuh, boys, is they ain't no such thing as the fastest gun in the West. Yes! *That's* what I'm tryin tuh say! Me and the Kid there, see, it jist happened like. It don't mean a thing. It . . . it's purty hard explainin it tuh yuh, boys, but it's important. It's very important . . .

> *He hesitates, losing it again, rubs his face in an effort to clear his head. He gazes down on the six-shooters on his hips, cups his hands as though to draw.* COWPOKES *and* BELLES *shrink away as though getting ready to duck for cover. But* THE SHERIFF *doesn't draw; he looks up blearily and proceeds with his revelations.*

SHERIFF: Right. The fastest gun. Tellin yuh about that. The fastest gun, well, we jist make all that up. See, yuh gotta learn that. I seen it soon as I seen the Kid go down. If somebody'd only told the Kid, why, mighta saved his life. Now . . . now, I know how bad you wanna believe it. I ain't no different, boys, I wanna believe it, too. I mean, I understand about why you're fixin me up in the Kid's duds, cuz it's somethin important tuh yuh, and yuh don't wanna lose it, I know. And I like these duds. I like how yuh think a me now. Shucks, Belle, you never even looked at me before, and . . . I mean, it'd be easy for me tuh pretend, tuh take yuh all in, make yuh think I'm somethin I ain't, and all the easier cuz it's what yuh *want* me tuh do! Yuh think yuh *need* it. But you're wrong, boys! Yuh gotta face up to it! I don't wanna hurt yuh, but I love this town, and sometimes, why, sometimes love hurts, don't it? Sometimes love makes yuh—

DEPUTY: (*interrupting coldly*) Shut up, Sheriff.

SHERIFF: Hunh?

DEPUTY: (*stepping forward to confront* THE SHERIFF) I said, shut yer fuckin mouth!

SHERIFF: (*confused, hurt*) Lissen, it ain't I ain't grateful—

DEPUTY: Sheriff, gimme them side-irons.

SHERIFF: Hunh? Yuh mean the Kid's—? (*Smiling hopefully:*) Sure, sure! That was jist what I was wantin tuh—

> As soon as THE SHERIFF *reaches for the guns, they*
> *blast away and* THE DEPUTY *spins and crashes to the*
> *floor.* THE SHERIFF *lets go the six-shooters, still in*

their holsters, stares in shock at the dying DEPUTY, *then in wonderment at his own hands.*

COWPOKE 212: Good gawdamighty! Did yuh see that!

COWPOKE 213: His own Deppity!

COWPOKE 214: Right between the fuckin eyes!

COWPOKE 215: Greased lightnin, man!

SHERIFF: (*still in awe at his own hands*) That . . . that's not what I—

COWPOKE 216: (*loud and commanding, as though suddenly taken aback*) Whoa there! Hey! Stand back, you jaspers!

COWPOKE 217: Hunh?

COWPOKE 218: What the—!

COWPOKE 216: (*again*) You see what *I* see?

COWPOKE 219: (*in overdrawn astonishment*) Well, I'll be horn-swoggled! It ain't the Sheriff at all!

COWPOKE 220: The Kid!

COWPOKE 221: It's the Kid hisself!

COWPOKE 222: THE KID'S COME BACK!!

A BELLE *screams. The* COWPOKES *fall back, leaving* THE SHERIFF *alone and perplexed, gazing down on the dead* DEPUTY. *He looks up, deeply pained.*

SHERIFF: This . . . this ain't it at all, fellas! I . . . I don't—

COWPOKE 223: J–just t–take it easy now, K–K–Kid!

COWPOKE 224: We're jist plain folks . . .

COWPOKE 225: Decent and law-abidin, Kid!

COWPOKE 226: Cain't shoot worth a damn!

COWPOKE 227: We ain't aimin tuh cause yuh no t-trouble, Kid!

COWPOKE 228: Jist take anything yuh want, Kid, only d-don't shoot!

COWPOKE 229: Don't sh-shoot—!

SHERIFF: Now, wait a damn minute—!

COWPOKE 230: Ain't nobody gonna t-try yuh, Kid!

COWPOKE 231: We know you're the f-fastest gun in the W-W-West!

SHERIFF: No! (*Flings away* THE KID's *hat.*) Goldurn it! Yuh gotta LISSEN tuh me, men! (*Flings away* THE KID's *gloves.*) Don't yuh reckanize me? Cain't yuh see I'm the man yuh elected—

> THE SHERIFF *draws the pistols to fling them away, but as soon as they're out of their holsters, they start blasting away.* COWPOKES *and* BELLES *dive for cover, some of them jerking and crumpling as though gunned down. Glass shatters, bullets whine, bells ring, women scream, horses whinny, hooves clatter, Indians yowl, barrels crash and rumble, etc., as the silver six-shooters blast away. As suddenly,*

they are silent. THE SHERIFF *drops them to the floor.*

SHERIFF: (*in anguish*) Yuh wouldn't lissen! Yuh wouldn't LISSEN tuh me!

The remaining COWPOKES *and* BELLES *creep out of hiding, slip forward, encircle* THE SHERIFF, *restrain him.*

COWPOKE 232: Easy now, Kid!

COWPOKE 233: Yore killin days is over, Kid!

COWPOKE 234: Brang the rope, Belle!

SHERIFF: Yuh wouldn't lissen . . . !

COWPOKE 235: We heard what yuh got tuh say, Kid. We cain't wait no longer.

COWPOKE 236: Some of us is dead, Kid, from waitin too long already.

COWPOKE 237: We cain't take no chances, Kid. You understand.

SHERIFF: I thought, if I could jist git the Kid, everything'd be okay . . .

COWPOKE 238: It's the end of the road, Kid.

COWPOKE 239: The end of the rope.

A BELLE *comes forward with a rope, and they prepare to string* THE SHERIFF *up from a rafter in the saloon. With the noose around his neck, he blurts out:*

SHERIFF: But wait! Why . . . why ME?

COWPOKE 240: Why? (*Pause.*) I'll tell yuh why. Because you're *dumb*, Sheriff. Because you're *dumb.*

SHERIFF: *But I don't wanna die! I been a good man, boys! I loved this town! I don't wanna—ACKK!*

> *As* THE SHERIFF *jerks and dances at the end of the rope, the* BELLES *and* COWPOKES *step forward to sing "They Day They Strung Up The Kid." This is hillbilly gospel singing, full of pathos and energy and triumph. It is sung mainly in full chorus, with four solo verses, preferably sung by four different persons, including at least one of the* BELLES *and* THE DEPUTY—*who, along with the other* COW-POKES *and* BELLES *who have fallen (but not* THE KID), *now rise and join in. One of the* COWPOKES *pulls his gun while the guitars are warming up and shoots* THE SHERIFF *in the belly to stop him jerking around.*

THE DAY THAT THEY STRUNG UP THE KID

Let us study the Kid's wondrous story!
Ain't nobody ever done what he did!
The West was a place a grace and glory
Till the day that they strung up the Kid!

SOLO: He was mean, he was magic, he was real!
Sweet Jesus, he was somethin tuh see!

He was white as the lilies a the field,
And as pure and as wild and as free!

SOLO: He taught us that a man must live fer beauty!
You ain't worth shit if you're only second best!
The law ain't nuthin but the guy who's fastest shootin!
If millions croak, well, that's the legend a the West!

So jist reflect upon the Kid's wondrous story!
Ain't no cowpoke ever done what he did!
The West was a place a grace and glory
Till the day that they strung up the Kid!

SOLO: He gunned down moralists and misfits and merchants!
Egalitarians he ground up fer manure!
He cleansed the country a philosophers and virgins,
And robbed the rich, and jist fer fun shot up the poor!

SOLO: But though they hung him up and blew his balls tuh heaven,
His story, they say, may not be done!
They say the world will be his tuh fuck forever!
For the Spirit a the West goes marchin on!

So bethink yuh of the Kid's wondrous story!
Ain't no cowboy ever done what he did!
The West will EVER be a place a grace and glory,
Since the day that they strung up the Kid!

LOVE SCENE

Lights come up on an empty stage. A young man and young woman enter separately right and left, stand opposite each other across the stage, hands at their sides, heads down, preferably at some distance. They are dressed simply, the man perhaps in shirt and slacks, the woman in blouse and skirt. They show no expression whatsoever throughout the entire performance—neither enthusiasm nor sullenness, neither excitement nor disgust, neither belligerence nor boredom. Their movements, while relaxed and natural, are minimal and reveal nothing, celebrate nothing. After a pause, they both raise their heads slowly until their eyes meet. They regard each other awhile, then begin moving toward each other, taking one or two steps before they are interrupted by an amplified voice. This voice is resonant, rich, capable of all sorts of mood shifts. It can come from anywhere in the auditorium, but preferably from somewhere above the actors.

VOICE: (*breaking in abruptly*): Hold it! Hold it!

> *The man and woman stop, look toward the voice source.*

VOICE: (*gently*) Uh, that's not quite the idea, I'm afraid. It's very important how we get started here, we don't just lock tired eyeballs and set out, team. You've got to get something of the old spiritual fire in it, the life of man, the fatal shafts, remember? I mean, you're not picking out a can of sardines in a supermarket, there's something happening here, and you have to project that somehow. All right, I'm sorry I started you so cold there, let's back it up and try it from the beginning again.

They step back, take their former positions, heads down, hands at their sides. After a brief pause, they lift their heads slowly until their eyes meet. They gaze at each other a moment and seem about to move forward again, when they are again interrupted.

VOICE: No. No, I'm sorry, you still don't have it. What can I tell you? There's something new about to happen here, something exciting, don't you feel that? It's what makes the world go round, light from heaven, that sort of thing. The sacred flame. Magic in the air and every dream comes true, right? Okay, now, forget what your mothers told you, listen to your appetites, trust in your hopes, and give it another whirl there.

They lower their heads, pause, then raise them slowly until their eyes meet. The voice sighs unhappily. They glance up toward the source, listen.

VOICE: Hunh-unh.

They lower their heads.

VOICE: You know, sometimes we get the wrong idea about this kind of experience. So much gets said about pattern and inevitability that you think you're being victimized or something when it comes your turn. Well, forget all that! Forget it! It's not like that! I'm telling you, damn it, *it's new!* Now, try it again!

They raise their heads slowly.

VOICE: No, no, no, no, *no!*

They lower their heads, listen.

VOICE: This is a discovery! a revelation! Don't any of these words *mean* anything to you? We're doing a romance, my friends, golden dreams, light from heaven, you can see that, can't you? When you look up there, we need the sound of trumpets. Hearts beating, thumpety-thump, joy unspeakable and full of glory—do you follow? All right then, one more time!

Slowly they raise their heads.

VOICE: No, no, that's awful, that's terrible!

They lower their heads.

VOICE: I tell you what, would it help if I told a story? Would you like me to fill it in a little, do you need some pictures, something to hang onto?

They look up toward the voice source, listen.

VOICE: All right, let's suppose there are crowds of people around, okay? Thousands of dull thick stupid people. You know them and you don't know them, they're just fixtures, been there all your life, you don't even see them anymore, you could do without them, but you don't much care. That's life, you say. You shuffle along with them, get pushed and push back, what does it matter, just get it over with. And then, suddenly, out there, on the streets, or maybe in the meadow, or on the bus, in the choir, it's not important, wherever you like, across the bar, on a castle drawbridge—in fact, when it happens, it all drops away anyway, you don't know where you are, you don't care, you just look up, and POWEE! there's this one face, this one person! Oh man, it's magic, it's a message, the world turns green, or pink, whatever, angels sing, the sun comes out, bells ring—okay: *take it!*

They lower their heads, pause, raise them slowly to stare again at each other as before.

VOICE: (*snappishly*) You call that ringing bells? Jesus.

They look down.

VOICE: *AGAIN!*

They raise their heads.

VOICE: No, goddamn it, *NO!*

They lower their heads.

VOICE: I'm sorry.

They look up toward the source.

VOICE: Look, think of it any way you like, any way that'll help. How about this: you've always wanted a red

wagon, right? It's the only thing you want in the whole
world and you can't have it. No, they say. No red
wagon! And then, you wake up Christmas morning, and
there, under the tree, there it is: a red wagon! Can you
feel that? Okay, again now!

*They lower their heads, pause, then raise them slowly
as before.*

VOICE: Look, forget the wagon, that was a mistake.

They look down.

VOICE: I don't know, maybe you could try being somebody
else, would that help? I'd hoped we could make something
brand new here, something all our own, but maybe that's
not fair. I can't expect you to come out of pure darkness,
can I? No. The world's got to you, of course it has, we
have to live with that, I understand. So, all right . . . let
me think . . . I know, how about the Paris and Helen
thing, do you know that one? It's pretty good, got the feel
of spring in it, fresh wine, the slaughter of lambs, it ought
to work. Okay then, try to put yourself there, in the scene,
ancient Greece, Athens in all its glory, beardy philosophers
in the busy marketplace and shepherds crooning away on
the hillsides, ships at sea, nice young kids like yourselves
running around in nothing but laurel wreaths . . . and into
it all, here come Paris and Helen! Now, Paris has never
laid eyes on this girl before, remember? He turns away
from some old graybeard and—god in heaven! there she
is!

Pause.

VOICE: You don't feel that. Mmm. All right, what about Abelard and Heloise? No? Caesar and Cleopatra? The Brownings? Uh . . . hey, wait, I've got it! Adam and Eve! Why not? That's easy! I mean, if we're going to succumb to the bad habits of the past, we might as well go straight for the heart, the core, am I right? So we've got the old garden then, the trees, the birds and bees, it's all very lush, very steamy and pent-up, are you with me? The glad season, summer morn, ripe for exploits and mighty enterprises—oh yes, this is good, this is very good! It's not that you're complete strangers, yet it's as though you'd never really seen each other before! There's a new light in the garden! A new odor! Oh hell yes! You bite deep into that fantastic apple, look up—*GO!*

> *They raise their heads and look at each other as before.*

VOICE: *STOP!* STOP, stop, stop . . .

> *They glance toward the voice source.*

VOICE: (*with mounting anger*) I don't want guilt and habit, damn it, I don't want theology—I want EXCITEMENT! THRUST! IMPACT! I want desperate undertakings! I want it filled with fury! When you look up and connect, I want the place to *rock!*

> *They look down.*

VOICE: (*with forced restraint*) You're just . . . you're just there, see, dead in the world, and what a world, it's

hopeless, but you look up, and goddamn! you can't believe it! it's Jesus Christ! it's the Virgin Mary! it's Sonja
Henie! it's roses of sunshine, violets of dew! it's truth,
goddamn it! it's beauty! your soul's ambition! your life
in death! Oh holy joy, lock on! *Feel* it! *NOW!*

They look up at each other as before.

VOICE: (*approvingly*) Good! Good! You're getting there!
It's starting to happen! Again!

They lower their heads, pause, raise them as before.

VOICE: Yes! that's it! that's great! Again!

They lower their heads, pause, raise them as before.

VOICE: (*high-spirited*) You've got it! Don't stop now!
We're on our way at last! Keep it moving! The
approach . . .

They take a couple steps toward each other.

VOICE: *STOP!* Stop!

They stop.

VOICE: (*letdown*) Damn you, why'd you have to spoil it?

Pause.

VOICE: (*grumpily, all the way down now off his gathering
peak*) You don't look like two people in love, you look
like you're out taking a morning constitutional in order
to keep your bowels regular. You can do better than
that. Now, take it again.

They step back, lower their heads.

VOICE: Skip that shit, we don't have all day, just look up and move!

They look at each other, take a couple steps forward.

VOICE: No, no, that's not it at all!

They stop, step back, look toward the voice source.

VOICE: (*exercising self-restraint*) I'm pushing you, I'm sorry. It's just that this can be such a great thing, I guess I'm overanxious for the best part. Now listen, this is important, so stay with me. What's happening here, what's about to happen, is no accident, right? You're not just stumbling into each other, are you? Never mind what brought you here in the first place, here you are, you see each other, everything locks in place, and you start to move. Now, that space there between you has got to come alive, to become charged with necessity, with compulsion! I want to see the sparks fly! I don't want you to walk, I want you to get dragged across that space! Are you paying attention? Okay, now look up and . . .

They look at each other, take a couple steps forward.

VOICE: (*drily*) What's the matter, kids, shoes hurting your feet? Underwear too tight?

They stop, step back, lower their heads.

VOICE: Come on, this is a love scene, gang! This is the biggest thing in your life! This is the biggest thing in history! It's the pleasure that means all the world! It's the sweetest story ever told! It's chasing rainbows through heavens of blue!

They raise their heads, gaze at each other, as the voice continues.

VOICE: It's the whole goddamn saga of the western world! It's castles of dreams, finding the grail, music of the spheres! There's magic in the air, wizards, love potions, and Satan's ass! Come on! I want transcendence! immortal longings! I want inscrutable forces at work! Now, move it! Bee to the blossom! Moth to the flame!

They step forward, as before.

VOICE: That's it! Keep going! Yes! She's the one! He's the one!

They continue their approach.

VOICE: (*with mounting excitement*) Come on! Bring it home! Pull! PULL! Over the wastes! Through the storm! O'er hill and dale! Moving mountains! You're on the way! You're reaching heaven's open—

They meet and kiss. This kiss is a simple casual embrace, hands on each other's arms, mouths meeting —it is instantly interrupted.

VOICE: HEY! What the hell do you think you're doing!

They remain together, but part lips and look toward the voice.

VOICE: Back up there, goddamn it!

They part, take a step or two backwards, still looking toward the voice source.

VOICE: Okay, that's enough!

They stop, wait.

VOICE: (*a little breathless—even at his calmest, the voice is now considerably more agitated and exciteable than at the outset*) I'll tell you when, and not before! You left out the whole goddamn courtship sequence!

They look at each other.

VOICE: Try that shit again, you'll get creamed! I can destroy you, you little bastards, and don't forget it!

They look up at the source.

VOICE: Okay. Circle around there a little bit now. Don't worry, it's going to be all right, we've got lots of time, the first part's always the trickiest, we're past the worst. Come on, circle about!

They look at each other, circle around, exchanging places, stop.

VOICE: (*gloomily*) Oh boy oh boy oh boy. Let me tell you, kiddies, the universe is not exactly standing on its ear. What is it, am I using the wrong words? Did I tell you just to circle around? I'm sorry. Think about carousels, worlds out of control, a hall of mirrors where the closer you get the farther away you are! We want honied lies, the light fantastic, the stink of roses and flash of ornaments, hearts on fire, feet afloat, get it up now! Good times are comin'! *MOVE!*

They complete their circle about each other, moving as before, returning to their former positions, while the voice continues.

VOICE: What're you doing? You call that the mad whirl? You call that ballin' the jack? Oh, that's subtle, that's very subtle!

They stop, look up.

VOICE: (*explosively*) *But I want REALISM, goddamn it!*

They look at each other as before, commence to circle again.

VOICE: I want pricks to harden and juices to flow! We're on our way to a fuck not a funeral! Come on, baby! Get some rhythm in that ass, show it to him, whaddaya think you got one for? Let's have it! Lemme *see* it! Lemme *feel* it!

They continue to circle about each other, around and around, without expression, always keeping the same distance, as the voice continues.

VOICE: I want tension! vibrations! heat! harmony! mysticism and melodrama! the feast of reason and the flow of soul! Come on! You're swinging now, but it's not crazy

enough! Get some grace in it! Get some evil! I want appetite and cruelty! joy and devastation! sin and suffering! That's it! Good! Now! *Home! GO!*

>*They stop and kiss, as before.*

VOICE: HOLD IT! . . . Too soon!

>*They stop kissing, look toward the voice.*

VOICE: (*still exceedingly excited, but holding himself back*)
Back it up! Back it up!

>*They step back to the circling distance, still looking
toward the voice.*

VOICE: (*with forced calm*) We're rushing it. We have to do
more here to prepare the way, or we'll lose it. Here's
where we make it or break it, this is our story, not the
rest of it, we invented tragedy and it happened right
here, let's not mock it. We're making it too easy, that's
the trouble. Not just attraction, remember, but resistance, too. Push, pull, push, pull. Got it? You want it
and you don't want it. You're excited and you're scared.
You're reaching out, but you like being alone. Go on.
Try it now.

>*They look at each other and begin to circle again,
as before.*

VOICE: (*continuing*) You know how good it's going to feel,
but it's probably going to hurt, too. Sensations sweet
and all that, you've heard the stories, but the stink of
death as well, the storm of terror. Joy and desolation,

push, pull, push, pull. Are you with me? You know it's going to happen, it has to happen, but you also know it's impossible. The whole world's watching. You don't care. Not in *here*, they say, not in church! Not in the middle of the street! But you can't wait! Lips like a honeycomb, mouth smoother than oil! Yum! Keep it up! Secret trysts! Forbidden gardens! A little tra-la-la there! a little Blue Danube, moonlight and madness, thick skirts and the flash of nimble ankles, hard thighs, snow-white bosoms, manly brows! Damn it, get some fire in it! Hunt! Flee! Why can't you make it go?

They continue to circle, round and round.

VOICE: (*with gathering gloom*) What's the matter with you? What's the matter with me? It's always worked before, why isn't it working now? Have I lost it? Is it over?

Pause, while the man and woman continue to circle silently about each other.

VOICE: (*mustering courage*) I tell you what, let's try the allegorical thing. Love embracing death, that kind of thing. The East and the West. Black and white. How about that?

They glance toward the voice source, continuing to circle, then watch each other again, as before.

VOICE: Right, black, and white, why not, should be good for something. The princess and the blackamoor. Hah! That thing he's got'll split you wide open, honey! She's old mother night herself, boy, full of sweet delirium and disease! Smell that black horniness? Smell that white corruption? Look at those chains! Look at those whips! By god, if we have time, if we hurry, maybe you can even go down on each other! Oh yeah, I'm feeling better now, this is pretty, this is primeval, this is depravity and virtue! We are getting there! We are on our way! This is the soul searching for body, conscience terrorized by the gonads! This is night and day! sun and moon! yin and yang! Get ready now! Oh boy! This is beauty and the beast, order and chaos, ego and id, we're up to our ears in it, *feel* it! God and the Devil! youth and age! terrific! the intrinsic and the extrinsic! it's a seduction! fight it! grab it! resist! surrender! It's man and society! zero and infinity! oh yeah! time and space! will and necessity! hot shit! it's war and peace! master and slave! *the beginning and the end! SYNTHESIZE!*

They stop circling, step forward and kiss, as before.

VOICE: (*at a high pitch of excitement, very frantic, very frustrated, coming down hard*) No, no, no, no, no, no, no . . . !

They part lips, look toward the voice source.

VOICE: (*nearly crying*) Oh goddamn, goddamn . . . !

A pause, while the voice makes an effort to get a grip on himself.

VOICE: You're not licking envelopes! You're not checking for fever! *You're in love!*

They kiss again.

VOICE: *LOOK AT ME!*

They part lips, look impassively toward the voice source.

VOICE: I'm telling you! This isn't some greasy old habit, this is brand new! Aren't you listening? This is Columbus at the edge of the world! Now, goddamn it, if you're about to fall off the damn world, you're going to *feel* something, aren't you?

They kiss.

VOICE: (*continuing*) Now put something into it! Put your life into it! Everything you've got! This is man in space! This is the soul at death's door! The backwards look toward the primitive terror, the leap in the dark, the thrust into truth and nature! Can't you get that? You've never been there before and you—

Pause.

VOICE: You *have* been there before, haven't you?

They part lips, look up toward the voice source.

VOICE: You bastards.

Pause. The man and woman continue to stare toward the voice.

VOICE: Well, fuck you. Forget all that, forget all you know, forget it! I said this was new, it's new! Come on! Mouth to mouth, damn it!

They kiss.

VOICE: (*continuing, peaking rapidly*) Eat her up! Suck him dry! I want action! Shock! Deception! Rape! Transfiguration! Come on! Make it weird! Damn it, kid, squeeze a little titty there, what do you think this is, the Middle Ages? Oh Jesus Christ, hurry up!

The man puts his hand casually on the woman's breast, as the kiss continues.

VOICE: (*still accelerating*) Get majesty in it! Panic! Redemption! Possession! Oh shit! Grab it! Go for it! Hurry! My god, are you still *kissing* each other? *JUMP HER, FOR CHRISSAKE!*

They stop kissing. The woman stretches out on the floor on her back. The man stoops down between her legs. They move indifferently, taking their time, as the voice raves on, nearly screaming now.

VOICE: GO! Make it mean! Make it dirty! You're children! Naughty! Behind the bushes. Peeking in your panties! An old man! Little girl! You're a priest and a nun! On the altar! Oh yeah! You're Brutus and Caesar! An old lady and her dog! Jesus and his Mom! Brother and sister! Oh goddamn! Luther and the Pope! Uf! Joan of Arc and the stake! Ah! George and Martha! In the cotton fields! Foo! On the floor of the Constitutional Convention! Blow him, baby! Bite him! He's death! He's God! He's the General! Oh hurry! Come on, boy, stick it in her deep! I want blood! I want grandeur! I want the slap of bellies and the roar of—WHAT THE HELL! *YOU STILL GOT YOUR CLOTHES ON, YOU DUMMIES!*

They look up toward the voice source.

VOICE: Get 'em off! Hurry! I MEAN NOW! *I CAN'T WAIT, GODDAMN IT!*

The man leans back, begins to unbutton his shirt.

VOICE: *Hers,* you fucking idiot, not yours! Move it, or you're dead! I swear to god, you're dead! Strip him, baby! Go! GO!

The man begins to unbutton the woman's blouse. She leans forward and works one of his shoes off. Etc.

VOICE: No! Can't wait! Tear it off! Faster! I'M TELLING YOU—*TEAR IT OFF!*

The man glances up at the voice, pauses momentarily, then proceeds to tear the woman's blouse.

VOICE: *(continuing)* Go! Rip! Kill! Oh! Come! Faster! Shit! Sorry! Ah! Please—*Aaahhhh* . . . . . .

Prolonged silence. The man and woman are still, methodically, routinely, ripping each other's clothes off.

VOICE: *(dully, still a little breathlessly, wearily, with stupefaction)* All right, knock it off, knock it off . . .

They glance uncertainly toward the voice, pause, rip just a little more.

VOICE: KNOCK IT OFF!

They stop ripping, sit quietly, attending the voice.

VOICE: Get your goddamn clothes on.

They reach for the torn blouse, skirt. They are still essentially impassive, as before, but there is a hint of growing tension.

VOICE: No, never mind.

They hesitate, drop the clothing, sit back.

VOICE: (*coldly*) You're through, you bastards, you know that.

They sit quietly, but glance at each other. A pause.

VOICE: (*not directly on-mike, but as though shouting into the wings*) Bring an Indian on!

Pause.

VOICE: I don't care, a Gook, a Red, the Mafia, Huns, Moors, hangmen, witches, zombies, pirates, whatever you've got back there! You got a spade technician? Okay, a spade technician, I don't give a shit, bring him on!

Pause.

VOICE: Deus ex machina, my ass! I want that nigger out here!

The man and woman draw together, watch the wings.

VOICE: (*still off-mike*) What do you mean, what does it mean? It don't mean a goddamn thing! It's realism, that's what it is! GET HIM OUT HERE!

A man wanders onstage (if not black, alter the relevant references). Like the man and woman, he is dressed casually, plays his part without enthusiasm or emotion. He carries a pistol, awkwardly, as though it has just been handed him. He turns to face the other two, who now stand in a crouch, clutching their torn clothing to their breasts.

VOICE: (*dully, on-mike again*) Shoot 'em.

The black man stands, hands at his sides, looking up toward the voice source. The man and woman, holding each other, edge away.

VOICE: You heard me! Shoot 'em, damn it!

The black man looks around for the voice, then gazes down without emotion at the other two. He does not raise the pistol.

VOICE: They're all used up. They're not worth shit anymore.

Pause. Three actors, as before.

VOICE: There they are, man, the whole western world, all that lunacy, all that history, *A* to Z—shoot 'em!

Pause.

VOICE: (*insistently*) Come on! You got no balls? IMAGI-NATION RULES THE WORLD, SHITHEAD! *LET 'EM HAVE IT!*

The black turns to go.

VOICE: (*pleading*) Wait! Wait a minute, goddamn it! At least—look, at least just point the gun at them, just that much, for god's sake . . . !

The black hesitates, shrugs, points the pistol more or less in the direction of the other two actors. They huddle together.

VOICE: (*flatly*) Bang. Bang, bang. Bang.

The actors glance hesitatingly toward the voice source, then move quietly offstage.

VOICE: Yeah. That's great. (*Fading:*) That's beautiful. (*Distantly:*) That's just beautiful . . .

Lights dim.

RIP AWAKE

Distant rumble of thunder. Enter Rip Van Winkle, more ancient than ever, toiling up a mountainside. He carries a jug, wallet, and old firelock. Another rumble of thunder: he pauses in his climb, sighs heavily, turns to the audience.

RIP:

There they go again, you hear them? Little buggers, they musta seen me coming, oh yes, got it in for old Rip, they do, probably got a big reception waiting for me up there!

> *He sits wearily on a stump, takes food from his wallet, uncorks the jug.*

You thought that last time was something—boy, you ain't seen nothing yet! That's what they're saying all right, that's what all that rumbling's about!

> *He eats and drinks, not with appetite, but nervously, killing time.*

Oh, there's a lot of power and magic up that mountain, you don't have to tell old Rip Van Winkle, he's been up there and seen it, that's a mean old buncha boys! But to hell with them, I'm going all the way tonight, swear to

God and old Henry, I ain't turning back, not this time, I've had enough!

> *Closer thunder. He pauses in his chewing, cocks an ear toward the sound, turns back to the audience.*

Oh, don't suppose I ain't scared! Old as I am, I ain't too old to be scared, no sir, you don't get that old! But finally, let me tell you this, finally being scared ain't the worst! No, it ain't, I've been through worse, much worse, and so scared or not, I'm going back up there tonight, I'm gonna bring this thing to what old Van Bummel used to call a con-su-mation! I ain't wasting another night!

> *He fails to convince himself entirely, takes another consoling pull on the jug, stands to pace.*

Just the same, though, I wish I didn't have to go up there alone. It don't seem to happen to nobody else like this, why am I always the one that gets left out and has to do everything by hisself? It ain't fair. Maybe if I hadn't slept through the Revolution, I wouldn't be needing one now. That one satisfied most everybody else. Of course, who says I'm going up there to raise hell, eh? Don't be too sure I ain't hoping to get stretched out amid the sassafras and witch-hazels for another twenty years, it could be. I mean, listen, I don't entirely regret them twenty years, I had some pretty glorious dreams, they come back and plague me now and again with hopes about the world I shouldn't be hoping—what I'm saying is: a game of ninepins and a flagon or two: what's wrong with that?

Distant thunder. He sits melancholically.

Just the same, I do wish I had old Wolf along for company at least. Ah: you noticed he ain't with me. Old faithful Wolf. Well, I shot him. That's right. I didn't mean to, no, it damn near broke my heart, it was them little Dutchmen's fault again. Boyoboy, those freaks have really messed up my life, me, old Rip Van Winkle, such a good old guy, it's sure hard to figure.

He hesitates, reflecting, then takes a meditative swig on the jug.

If it *was* old Wolf. Maybe it wasn't Wolf. Looked like Wolf. And we got on good enough, like I always done with Wolf, so that was good enough for me. That's the trouble with you, Rip, old Peter Vanderdonk used to say, that's just what's wrong with you. You don't distinguish things properlike, to you a fish is just a fish, a pole a pole, a tree a tree, that's what's wrong with your damn farm, you can't recognize the weeds from the cabbages, that's how you got stuck with such a devil of a wife, I bet you don't know your own kids when you see them!

He laughs at the memory of Peter Vanderdonk, then pauses to reflect.

Or was it Peter who said that? No, maybe it was Brom, probably it was Brom . . . or wasn't old Brom dead then? Well, it don't matter. It got said, that's what counts, it got said, and not a word of it true.

*He sighs ruefully, casts an uneasy glance back up
the mountain.*

Anyway, whether it was Wolf or not, I wish he was with
me, if I had old Wolf along I'd be up there by now. Shoot,
it wouldn't even have to be Wolf, anybody'd do, anything'd do . . .

*He jumps up as though inspired, starts to pack up
his food.*

Say, that's an idea! That's an idea! Maybe I oughta go
back down and see if I can't find me a dog somewhere . . .
or maybe one of you folks! I mean, what have you got to
lose, twenty years—

A sudden crack of thunder startles him.

Hey! Now, they didn't have to do that! You know, sometimes I get the idea they're just egging me on, teasing me
like, like they *want* me to come back up there, I don't
know why, it's like they want to get even with me for
something—though, shoot, that don't make proper sense:
it ain't old Rip's ever done nothing to *them!*

He reconsiders this, grins.

Except sneak me a couple swigs of their hollands, and look
where *that* got me! Oh, that flagon! that wicked flagon!

He laughs and drinks from his own jug.

Of course, when you come to think of it, I did kind of
steal their thunder, so to speak, didn't I? I mean, everybody's heard of Rip Van Winkle, ain't they? But as for them

little fellas off Captain Hudson's Half Moon, if it weren't
for old Rip, they'd be plumb forgot by now.

He brightens.

Hey! Maybe that's it! Yeah, maybe they've figured out
that it's the guys that get it done *to* them that get all the
credit, and maybe now they're hankering for their own
turn! Hah!

Thinking it over, his cheer fades. He sits again.

Not likely though. They probably don't even care about
such things, all high and mighty up on their mountain,
they've got their own silly game to fret about, and what
do they care for the rest of it, we just like to pretend
they're out to spook us. Shoot, I could be the goddamn
sheriff coming after them, and they wouldn't give a care,
they'd just think it was some kind of joke!

Distant thunder.

Wait! What am I saying? They wouldn't even think it
was a joke, not them guys, how could they, they ain't got
a sense of humor like you and me got, no, I've seen them,
you take it from old Rip, they ain't got no feelings of *any*
kind! Lord, that there game of ninepins I watched, I ain't
seen so much gloom since old Dominie Van Shaik first
come to these parts hooting and wailing about the horrors
of hell, which may I say in passing I hope has lived up to
his expectations! No, I tell you, that's one depressing outfit
up there, I took to drinking their liquor so as not to feel
like shooting myself!

He shudders, thinking about it, takes a pull on his own jug.

So why am I going back up there? I don't know. Maybe just to get another swig of that hollands, why not? Maybe I could sleep backwards, start all over. After what I've been through, anything is possible.

He starts to drink, is interrupted by another rumble of thunder. He leaps up irritably, commences to pace.

They ain't gonna let me alone, are they? They stole twenty of my best years, ruined my fowling piece, made me miss old Nick Vedder's wake and shoot my dog, and now they ain't even gonna let me die in peace!

He turns on the audience.

I mean, you think about it, just think how it'd be to go to sleep at—how old are you? twenty-five?—all right, and so you wake up and you're suddenly forty-five! You drop off in your late thirties, which ain't so young itself, and you come to already pushing sixty, how would that make *you* feel? All right, you say, but old Rip, he's different, what'd *he* have to lose, he was born old, you say— well, that just goes to show how bad things need straightening out around here! Or else, he's something special, you say, look at all that glory it got him, what's he complaining about, why, he oughta be taking presents up that mountain, what's twenty years if you can go down in history? Well, that so-called glory, that so-called history, let me tell you, that's something I could damn well do without!

He pauses for emphasis, takes a determined pull on the jug.

Oh, all right, I admit it, it was kinda fun. At first. I mean, it was something of a sensation there for a little spell, and I got a kick out of relating my story down at Nick's inn— or I mean, the Union Hotel, Nick was dead—and *it's* gone, too, you know, the Hotel, yes, ain't nothing stands long on this earth, not around here! Well, like I say, I enjoyed telling the story, what there was of it to tell, mostly about that dismal bowling party them weird little dwarfs was throwing, and then that first shock of coming to town again after twenty years, but it didn't take all that much in the telling, nobody wanted to hear the longer part about the dreams, and all too soon it was an *old* story—aw, shut up, Rip, they'd say, we heard that one before—and meanwhile, I was having other problems.

He listens to the distant thunder, sits again on the stump, continues.

For one thing, I had laid me down feeling fit, never mind what you might've been told, and I had woke up to a whole lot of misery and decrepitude! Why, just consider what can happen to your teeth in twenty years of unattended rot—took me a week just to scrape all the moss off, find out which ones was still in there, not many, two, three. And you go shift your old center of gravity for that long a stretch, you'll soon see it ain't all that easy to get upright again, I kept tipping over like a keg with a false bottom—oh, I know what you're thinking, you're thinking: lucky for old Rip, he'd been practicing that supine position so many years running, it probably come natural to him, good for his health. Well, you're wrong. I'd heard it said about having the starch took out of you, but I never knew properly what it meant till I tried to get up that day and get everything functioning again. Even my bones were soft and my old kidneys had just quit working altogether, I don't mention worse things. And my muscles! Not only were they gone to flab, but I'd slept on my back all them twenty years, and they'd sort of sunk away to the rear— oh, I was a pretty unusual specimen there for several years, I ain't all that famous a beauty now!

> *He drinks, listening meditatively to the distant thunder.*

And they tell you how long my beard had grown, but they don't mention how my toenails had grown right through my boots, some of them, the rest curled round and grew into my feet, I can't figure out to this day how I was able to walk down that mountain, I had to cut my damn boots off and I only got seven toes to this day, crocodiles got prettier feet than I got! And even that wasn't the worst of it!

> *Glancing uneasily up the mountain, as though afraid of being overheard, he leans forward, becomes more intimate.*

The worst was, you see, I couldn't get really awake after. I was half asleep all the day long. After losing twenty years,

I was scared to death of falling asleep ever again, but damn it, I kept dropping off just the same. I just couldn't get my head clear, maybe it was on account of my brains had sunk to the back of my head or something, I don't know, but I kept drifting off, and I couldn't tell whether I was awake or dreaming—I kept trying to wake up even when sometimes I probably *was* awake! You know how when you're sleeping and the cock starts crowing, or the baby's crying, or the bells are ringing, or somebody's at the door, and you know you oughta get up, but there's something inside you, way down inside you, it ain't you, not exactly, it's something or somebody you live with in there, and it's smarter than you, smart as you think you are, it's smarter, and it don't want to get up, so it starts changing things, I don't know how it does it, it turns the bells into a bobsled and you go off for a holiday, it takes you to the door, opens it up, there's an old friend you ain't seen in years, he comes in, there's a party, stories about the old times, you go off together, have a pint, come back, days pass, you go to bed, get up, go to bed, get up, and down at the tavern somebody says: Hey, Rip, I come by and knocked this morning, how come you didn't answer? Well, that's how it was with me all day long, all night long, for weeks, years maybe, I lost all track.

He stands, begins to pace.

I tried to walk it off. I'd walk for miles, I'd walk till I couldn't walk no more, trying to shake it off, get my head put straight, or maybe I only dreamt I walked, I couldn't never tell, sometimes I had bunions and blisters, sometimes

I didn't. I tried to starve myself awake, I gave up drinking, gave up eating, only to wake up down at the Union Hotel with a pint and a chickenleg in my hands, talking to Nick Vedder who'd been dead nigh onto twenty years. I'd get to thinking about that, about how it couldn't be Nick, and sure enough it'd be my old friend Brom Dutcher. Brom, I'd say, Brom! By god, Brom, let me buy you a beer! I thought you got killed in the war, I thought you got killed at the storming of Stony Point, they told me—No, Rip, he'd say, they just made all that up, you know how Peter is, he's got to have all the ends tidied up! And we'd laugh, thinking about old Peter Vanderdonk, and Jonathan'd come out and join us, Jonathan Doolittle, there on the bench where that old tree used to stand, and I'd say, well, Brom, goddamn it, tell us, what *really* happened? And he'd laugh and say, well, I got drowned in a squall at the foot of Antony's Nose, Rip.

He stops, staggers backwards.

Oh no, Brom!

He covers his face.

Who you talking to, Rip?

He looks up as though surprised, confused.

Hunh? Oh, sorry, Peter, I'd say, it'd be Peter Vanderdonk asking that, I must have dozed off there a minute, Peter, I thought you was old Brom Dutcher! Just so's we get our facts straight, Rip, he'd say, and we'd both laugh at that, if that's what I was doing, laughing, and he'd buy me a pint.

No, hold on, Peter, I'd say, I'm laying off that stuff, I got to get straightened out, but he'd say, one beer ain't gonna hurt you none, Rip, you ain't had nothing to eat nor drink for two weeks now, you've got to get a little strength back. So, okay, I'd drink it—and oh! it was good! Why, Peter, I ain't had beer like this since before the Revolution! And he'd look at me queerlike and say: What're you talking about, Rip? What revolution?

He slumps to the stump, beginning to weep.

And I'd wake up, alongside the river, a fishing pole in my hands instead of the beermug, and Dame Van Winkle pulling my ear and hollering at me to get back to my chores. Well now, I knew *she* was dead, I'd been there when she burst a blood vessel in a fit of wrath and contentiousness at that bowlegged peddler from New England—oh, I know what you're thinking, that was supposed to have happened while I was up the mountain, right? Well, that's true, it did—but just the same, I was there, I saw that blood vessel pop, saw that wheyface peddler running down the road, I'm telling you, the old blatherclack cocked up her toes and keeled over right in my arms, and you know what her last words were? This is how I *know* I was there. Her last words were: Rip, in the name of Jesus H. Christ, button up your fly!

He breaks down in tears.

So, see, I knew she was dead, I knew it couldn't be her pulling on my ear like that, so I socked her on the head with my fishing pole and threw her in the river—get out

of my wretched life, woman, once and for all! I hollered.
Lord, I'd been wanting to do that for years, I felt as joyful
as I'd felt since ever I dipped into that wicked flagon!
Whoopee! And then, as she drifted away there, just under
the water, I saw it wasn't that evil old wife of mine, after
all, no, it was my daughter Judith, my own little girl, my
dear little girl, oh my God, what has become of me . . . ?

*He is sobbing uncontrollably. Slowly, with effort,
he recovers, blows his nose loudly.*

And it was about that time, I think it must have been about
that same time, when I shot poor Wolf. We were out
hunting, I saw this beautiful stag . . . well, you can guess
easy enough how that one turned out. But by then, I'd got
so used to things turning into other things, I just went on
supposing Wolf *was* a stag, and I took him home and ate
him, kept waiting for old Wolf to turn up again at the
door. But he never did. He never did.

He pauses, reflecting, turns slowly to the audience.

And then, early one morning, at exactly 4 A.M., I woke up.
I heard them four bells, and each one of them was like the
steps of a ladder. Up I come.

He rises from the stump as he counts.

One. Two. Three. Four. On the fourth one I was awake
like I'd never been awake before. My nose was snorting,
my hands clawing, my eyes were starting out of my head!
There was a half moon out, not bright enough to make
things look like day, I ain't going to exaggerate it none,

but it was bright enough for me to see the edge on everything. I saw my four walls, my bedposts, my old wreck of
a body, like I was seeing them for the first time. My heart
was pounding away ninety miles an hour, and my mouth
was dry as a bone. The lumps in the mattress nudged me, I
heard every rustle of the straw, it was so clear, I thought it
was trying to tell me something. Cracks on the wall, webs
on the windowpane, the rough edge on the floorboards,
dents in the kettle, I saw it, I felt it all. I was all atremble, I
was seeing too much, I could see how everything was put
together like, I could see all the specks in my body, what
did old Van Bummel call them? I forget, but I could see
them, each and every one, dancing around like crazy, everything was like that, oh, I was awake all right, I was
really awake! And after that . . . I never fell asleep again.

He pauses, takes a long pull on the jug, starts to sit.
A loud rumble of thunder puts him on his feet
again.

All right, all right, I'm coming, hang onto your britches! I
don't know why they're so allfired anxious to get me up
there, for all they know I'm coming to whup their fat little
arses, and well I might, too, I got cause enough!

He glances up at the audience.

Ah, but hold on there, you're saying, wait just a dadblame
minute! I know what you're thinking, you're thinking, old
Rip Van Winkle, why he's one of them happy mortals of
foolish well-oilt dispositions, which take the world easy,
eat white bread or brown, he ain't got it in him to whup

nobody's arse, that's what you're thinking, ain't it? Sure, we know what old Rip's like, he's that lovable local character from the little village of yellow brick houses and great antiquity down there at the foot of these here fairy mountains, so-called—old Rip, who helped everybody else with their chores but never done his own, fooled away his days at Nick Vedder's inn, fished with a rod as long and heavy as a Chinaman's whatsit, and let old Dame Van Winkle wear the family galligaskins! Yes, I know, I know —it's like old Peter Vanderdonk used to say to me: you're a national heritage, Rip, he'd say, don't go spoiling it! Huh! Well, his grampaw was a historian, and old Peter bless his heart wasn't all that right in the head hisself. I mean, I'll tell you something, I ain't all that sure I *am* old Rip, I might be young Rip, or even little Rip, for that matter, my own grandson! I mean, look at the times we're living in, it don't hardly make sense that old Rip could still be around, does it? Or shoot, maybe my name ain't even Rip Van Winkle, that's possible, maybe old Peter made it up, laid it on me that day he saw me come down off the mountain, what do *I* know? Maybe *I'm* Peter Vanderdonk, maybe I've been living with my stories so long I've got senile and started believing them—oh, it ain't easy to grow old, you've got to do something to keep your mind off it . . .

> *A sudden crack of thunder makes him wince. He drinks. The jug is nearly empty.*

I mean, just take that morning I woke up, that morning I really woke up at last, for good and all. You can imagine how jumpy I was, all full of joy and fright at the same time, I walked the floor till daybreak, listening to the blood pounding in my ears, and then I rushed out to tell everybody the good news: old Rip Van Winkle has woke up at last! The first folks I run into, they just looked at me like, oh oh! look out, something wrong with that old boy! But they were strangers, I just gave them all a hug and left them gaping, went looking for my friends, wait till old Peter hears about it, I'm thinking—Peter! I've woke up, it's okay! But I couldn't find Peter. I couldn't even find anybody who'd ever heard of Peter Vanderdonk. Maybe he's down at the Union Hotel, I thought. But when I got there, there wasn't any Union Hotel, just some kind of fancy dispensary or other. George the Third, General Washington, they were gone. The bench. But the tree was back, though. Weird.

He takes another long guzzle, emptying the jug.

Well, I've been looking for my old friends ever since. Can't find a one of them. I'm all alone. Got left behind. Like always. And I've been trying to get back to sleep again, too. Can't. Just once, I think, just for ten minutes. Can't.

Wearied reflective pause.

Yep, them little fellas off the Half Moon, they made a mess out of me, they done a proper job of it!

He sits. Sudden loud clap of thunder; he starts up off the stump again, glares resentfully up the mountain.

Lord, you'd think they'd have more consideration for their own kinfolk, wouldn't you? I mean, one of them may be a Van Winkle for all I know, how else did they know my name? Still, maybe they've forgot about being kin, maybe they've been up on that mountain playing that drunken game of theirs too long—I mean, it's true, you can't hardly recognize them anymore with their funny red faces, feathered hats, and high-heeled shoes. It's like what happens to mountain people everywhere, I reckon. Steal their balls from them, that's what they need, give them something else to think about, might quiet things down around here, too, good idea.

> *He tips the jug, discovers it is empty, throws it away in disappointment.*

Oh boy. Now I'm alone, now I'm really alone! And I'm so tired, I'm so damn tired, so weary of seeing how things are, you see it once, you've seen it for all time, I just want to doze off for a week or two, yum. You know, that long time when I couldn't get awake, it was pretty awful, but not being able to get to sleep, that's worse. I mean, even though it's pretty spooky having things turning into other things all the time, it did have its sweet side—but there ain't *no* relief from having to watch things turning into themselves, that's the spookiest of all! All them little specks, trying to get free—whew! Listen: all them fancy words that Peter and old Van Bummel the schoolmaster talked, all the silly stuff that Dominie preached, it all comes down to one thing: trying to keep them goddamn specks from blowing apart. I'm telling you the truth now!

Well, I figured after a few weeks of it, I'd had enough. I was an old man and I'd had enough. Rip, says I, Rip, it's time to let go! Blast away! So I let go. And that was when I discovered that weird little critter living inside me was still down there, that bugger that wouldn't let me wake up, now he wouldn't let me blow, I could let go all I wanted, he was having no part of it. Now, I ain't blaming them old boys from the Half Moon up there for putting him there, I got a fair suspicion they didn't have nothing to do with it, he was probably down there all the time, tending his own business, so to speak—no, in fact, the way I figure it, it was old Rip they invented, old Rip Van Winkle they conjured up in that flagon of hollands, and *that's* where all the trouble started!

He is getting carried away by enthusiasm.

Now, *that's* what I've been trying to tell you about, that's why I've got to go back up there! Oh, I ain't expecting no miracles, I ain't expecting to come back down the mountain, if I *do* come down, like I was before I first clumb up, I wouldn't even *want* to come down like that, so dumb and innocent like I was, I'd just get in trouble all over again! But, by damn, we have to balance things out, them old Dutchmen and me, they botched up my life something awful with that flagon of sweet dreams, they've got to share that gin around a little now, I'm too old to keep on living a stranger to myself and kin, we're gonna come to some kind of peace and understanding, or ninepins ain't the only things gonna come rolling down this mountain!

Loud crack of thunder. He jumps, shrinks away, his bravado rapidly fading.

Whoo! Listen to that! Aw, you must be crazy, Rip! Who're you kidding? Out of food and liquor, et your dog, and toting an old firelock that won't even fire no more, why don't you go back home, you decrepit old ninnyhammer?

He pauses, reflecting, answers himself.

Why? Because I ain't got a home no more, that's why. I don't know where it is. Used to be there. Ain't there anymore. I can see everything clear as a damn bell, and I can't see my own home! Maybe . . . maybe I ain't never really had one, or maybe it was off someplace else, I seem to remember one okay, parts of one anyhow . . . but maybe Peter or somebody just stuffed them pictures of a home in my head somehow, Lord knows it gave in to a lot of stuffing! Or else, maybe you can only see it when you're half asleep, I mean, a lot of things have disappeared since I woke up, a lot of my *favorite* things, I should say, and the ways you used to could see things clinging together, all gone now—oh, it was a damn sight more comfortable when I could see just what I wanted to see!

He gazes unhappily back up the mountain, listens to thunder, more distant than the last, braces himself for the trip, putting a brave face on it.

All right, come on, Rip, don't just stand around here and get killt for nothing, let's get it over with!

He turns to the audience, in parting.

Look, do me a favor though, will you? If you come across old Peter Vanderdonk, why, tell him you've seen old Rip, he's wide awake, tell him that, tell him he ain't sleeping through no more Revolutions, tell him he don't know who he is or what's been happening to him, but he knows he ain't taking no more static from them runts off the Half Moon! That's it! Tell Peter his old national heritage was last seen proceeding back up the mountain to rassel with the spooks in his life! Hah! And one more thing: tell him there was two main differences from when he clumb up there the first time—he still had all his teeth and ten good toes then, and that first time he was so dumb, he thought that what he was doing, he was doing of his own sweet pleasure! Tell him that!

> *He smiles grimly, exits, toiling up the mountain. There is a flash of light and a sudden terrific thunderclap.*

A THEOLOGICAL POSITION

for and with Gail Godwin

CHARACTERS

Priest
Man
Woman

A plain room with wooden stools and a large rustic table, bearing a pitcher of wine, glasses, bread and knife, bowl of fruit. The PRIEST, *in black miter and cassock, gold chains and pendants, is pacing the floor pompously, concluding a declamation. The* WOMAN *sits on a stool with her hands folded in her lap, drawn into herself, smiling politely, obviously pregnant. The* MAN *sits near her, protectively; he seems troubled, faintly belligerent, as he attends the* PRIEST.

PRIEST: (*with finality*) Then, I have made our position clear.

MAN: Sure. I knew about all that without you telling me.

PRIEST: Aha. Then, you are prepared to correct your ridiculous story!

MAN: (*hesitating, glancing at the* WOMAN) No.

PRIEST: But, you fool, I tell you it is impossible!

MAN: I know. That's what I thought, too.

PRIEST: (*pacing about with exasperation, gesturing broadly*) That's what you thought, that's what you thought!

> *He spins on the* MAN, *who is not looking at him.*

And what's more, it simply cannot be permitted! Do you understand? If what you say is true, which is impossible . . .

> *His gaze falls on the* WOMAN. *She looks up at him, smiles demurely. He softens, smiles weakly, then once more draws himself up, attempts without complete success to resume his former manner.*

If what you say is true . . . ahem, if what you say is true, well, certain . . . that is, I must advise you, certain drastic measures . . . ahem, you understand what I—?

MAN: (*standing, confronting the* PRIEST, *mouth set*) You won't hurt her.

> *The* PRIEST *shies, puts the table between himself and the* MAN.

I couldn't let you hurt her. But I'm not going to lie. I didn't want it to turn out like this, but I'm not going to lie.

> *The* MAN *stands behind the* WOMAN, *his hands on her shoulders. She smiles up at him, then gazes again into her own lap.*

PRIEST: (*pacing meditatively*) Our position is fixed.

MAN: Yes. Of course.

PRIEST: There's little we can do.

> *He glances up, but shies from the* MAN's *steady gaze.*

Still, there might be a way. Not exactly legal, of course.

> *The* MAN *looks dubious, but is prepared to negotiate.*

Yet, it would probably satisfy, literally, the statutes. You understand: I only wish to help.

MAN: Yes. I appreciate that.

PRIEST: Ahem. Well. The spirit of the law of course is absolutely transparent. It was intended to ascertain that no further, uh, events, yes, events of *that* sort, should ever occur again. Which, in view of the way things have turned out in the past, is certainly reasonable, don't you agree?

> *He pauses, leans his head toward the* MAN, *as toward a recalcitrant pupil, waits for him to nod assent, then continues his pacing. Throughout, the* MAN *is in obvious awe of the* PRIEST's *power and intellect, but at the same time instinctively suspicious of it. He wants to help, but is afraid of the possible consequences.*

Our position is theologically indisputable. First, we assert, we acknowledge, that such an occurrence is impossible, absolutely impossible! That is, not merely impossible spatially and temporally, but also impossible conceptually, suppositionally, inferentially, and expressively! Impossible *simpliciter!* Do you understand?

He pauses, leans again toward the MAN, *receives the nod, then continues his pacing, building up steam.*

It has in fact been our experience that every such claim dissolves sooner or later into a pack of silly lies, wishful fantasies of the peasant imagination. No offense, of course, but you people simply lack the historical knowledge to put such things as giants and fairies in perspective. More than one witch has gone to the stake, guilty of nothing more than serial discontinuities! More than one split belly has released only the fetor of exotic solecisms, syncretic projections! I hope I make myself clear!

The MAN, *who has winced at the "split belly," now nods reluctantly, keeping his steadfast gaze on the* PRIEST.

All right. But, secondly, *secondly*—and now I speak, *secundum quid*, as a theologian—the very idea of such an event is not only irrelevant to our experience of the transcendence, it is repugnant! It is regressive, infantile, depraved! It is, I tell you, seditious! What after all is the central message of all our revelations?

The MAN *stares blankly at the* PRIEST.

I'll tell you what it is! Rebirth! Regeneration! The new man! Out of obscurity and corruption into light! Freedom from nature!

MAN: But—!

PRIEST: Oh yes, reason and revelation may never intersect, it's true, but it's simply because they are parallel and complementary routes out of that same primeval forest toward man's total understanding of himself, toward that glorious destiny we can but faintly glimpse through our yet imperfect and muddied lenses! Are you listening to me? If the Word was made flesh, flesh has also absorbed and enriched the Word—but who among you speaks of the offspring, much less of that Consciousness who fathered this miracle—no, it's forever the magic bellies we go on reverencing, idolatrizing, the extravagant sow, the immaculate whore! Well, this must come to an end! Do you hear me?

MAN: Yes, but—

PRIEST: Oh, we are not trying to conjure away the misfortunate origins of all our sons, no, that is not what our mysteries portend, we wish only to liberate them from their primitive—and if I may be so blunt—their fetal attachments! So enough! I say here and now, there has never been such a conception, and there will never be another one again! *It stands to reason!*

He pauses, turning full upon the MAN.

Now finally, and I conclude, finally, and most important, the fixed point in our position: even if—and though impossible and demonic—it *should* occur, and I am here beyond the pale of admissible postulates, even

if it should occur: *we could not permit it! WE COULD
NOT PERMIT IT!* Do you hear me?

MAN: But I thought you said—

PRIEST: *DO YOU HEAR ME?*

MAN: (*submissively*) Yes . . .

PRIEST: We could not permit it! We could not permit it!
Not only would it be an intolerable interference in
human existence, *intolerable*, I tell you, it would be he-
retical! Yes, I do not hesitate to say it, it would constitute
an act of Divine Heresy, an act of perversion and historical depravity! Either we are in the guidance of a benev-
olent, progressive, and rational force, or we are
possessed by irresponsible demons and must resist! Thus,
and I need say no more, the law is obviously intended to
be preventative,, that is its spirit, that is the sacred resolve
behind its design! That is absolutely clear, I assume?

> *He pauses, awaits the uncertain nod, continues as
> before, though softening somewhat. He becomes
> more and more conscious of the* WOMAN's *presence.*

Right. *But*—and mind you, this is a rather tenuous
but—while the spirit of the law is utterly transparent,
the *letter* of the law is admittedly a bit, shall we say, ambiguous. Perhaps in fact it was meant to be ambiguous.
Yes, it was no doubt drafted at a time when the contin-
gency of certain, ah, deviltries (*he glances at the* WOMAN,
who smiles demurely back at him), now held to be, that
is to say, now known to be preposterous and unthink-

able, was still entertained, and thus was conceived as a cautionary and sanctifying use of the Devil's own invention, so to speak, ambiguity as a weapon in the service of salvation—but perhaps these are subtleties beyond your grasp—

The WOMAN *takes a deep breath, as though inflating her breasts, causing the* PRIEST *to catch his own breath.*

Yes, the . . . uh . . .

MAN: The letter, you were saying . . .

PRIEST: Yes, the letter. It, that is, ahem, it demands, it only demands . . .

He is very aware of the WOMAN. *She smiles warmly at him. He swallows, continues with difficulty.*

Well, how can I say, ah, the only proof, ahem, you understand I only wish to help, I am not myself fond of burnings, and she, well, I mean to say, the only . . . ah, that the *way* is not barred, do you understand? that there has been, well, that there has clearly *been*—do I make myself clear?

MAN: Sure. Penetration.

PRIEST: (*trying with difficulty to be matter-of-fact, self-consciously avoiding the* WOMAN's *placid gaze*) Yes.

MAN: Why didn't you just say so?

PRIEST: Well. I did . . .

MAN: Let's not beat around the bush. Penetration.

PRIEST: Yes. However, uh, however slight.

MAN: I understand.

PRIEST: (*as he sits, obviously relieved*) Well, then!

> *An awkward pause.*

MAN: Well, what?

PRIEST: (*irritably, not looking at the* MAN) Well . . . the obvious . . .

MAN: I don't get you.

> *The* PRIEST *springs to his feet, throwing his hands up in grand gestures of impatience with peasant stupidity, but continuing to avoid the* MAN's *steady gaze.*

PRIEST: My God, you people make me lose faith in the entire human enterprise! I don't get you, I don't get you! By heaven, if there's money to cross the palm, you get it quick enough, don't you! If there's a chance to be the talk of the neighborhood, the cock of the walk, yes, then you get it quick enough! Why, man, I mean you should just . . .

> *His storming about has carried him into confrontation with the* WOMAN. *She smiles. He falters. His voice softens.*

Well. That is, you should . . . ahem, you should . . . I, well, while I'm here, you know, so that I can see . . .

MAN: You mean—? Here? In front of you?

PRIEST: (*sitting, as though after some terrible ordeal*) Well, it would be proof . . .

MAN: You're crazy!

PRIEST: I'm only trying to help.

MAN: Anyway, it's too late. I mean, she's six months gone.

PRIEST: (*weakly*) Uh, well, the law doesn't say anything about when exactly. Not the letter.

MAN: (*laughing cynically*) You guys are really something!

> The PRIEST, *hardening, rises to go.*

PRIEST: All right, forget it. I don't know why I bother. What difference does it make to me? She will have to report to—

MAN: No, wait! I'm sorry!

> *He gathers strength, turns to gaze down at the* WOMAN.

I'll try.

> *The* PRIEST, *at the door, watches attentively. The* WOMAN *smiles at the* MAN. *The* MAN, *standing over her, rubs his hands nervously on his pants, shifts his weight from one foot to the other. He sighs.*

I can't do it. I just can't do it. Not like this.

PRIEST: Don't be a child, man! This is a serious matter!

MAN: I know, but I can't help it. I can't do it.

PRIEST: You're aware of the penalty?

MAN: (*meekly*) Yes.

PRIEST: For both of you!

MAN: Yes.

PRIEST: Hers are worse!

MAN: Wait! Maybe . . .

> *He peers down inside his pants.*

No. No . . .

PRIEST: (*exploding*) Good God, what am I doing here? Why do I betray this weakness? Here I risk my robes to help both of you out of this mess—!

MAN: Look, would it . . . would it matter who did it?

PRIEST: (*still blustering*) —And on a questionable technicality at that—and you behave like a damned fool! A child! Well, by heaven above, when the torch is lit, you'll see it go—what do you mean, would it matter . . . ?

MAN: You know, I mean would it be the same if someone else, you for instance, did it to her instead of me?

> *The* PRIEST's *fury collapses. He glances toward the* WOMAN. *She smiles.*

PRIEST: You mean, you want me to . . . that is, you're suggesting that I . . . ?

MAN: That's it. Would it be the same?

PRIEST: (*swallowing*) Well. Yes. Yes, I suppose. Why not? Why not? But, you mean, you don't mind if I . . . ?

MAN: No, go ahead.

PRIEST: No, *really*, that is—?

MAN: I said it was all right, it's all right.

PRIEST: Ah. Well.

> *He smoothes his robes, clears his throat, glances nervously at the* WOMAN.

Yes. Ahem. It's a bit irregular, of course.

MAN: Yes, but it's for her sake. I don't mind if you don't.

PRIEST: Still, it is entirely legal. Entirely legal, you understand.

MAN: Well then . . .

PRIEST: And there are precedents.

> *The* MAN, *silent, watches him.*

Certain precedents.

> *Pause. The* PRIEST *laughs drily, nervously.*

But you wouldn't, uh, well . . .

> *He glances about the room.*

Where do you think I should . . . we should . . . ?

MAN: The table?

PRIEST: Well! Why not?

> *He circles the table, rubbing his pale hands nervously, smiling uneasily, stealing glances at the* WOMAN.

Yes, yes, I'm sure it would do, strong enough, heh heh, of course—that is, how do you people say, when there isn't any other teapot in a tempest . . . ?

> *He laughs drily, swallows. The* WOMAN *smiles at him demurely, her hands folded in her lap.*

I mean to say, it's adequate, quite adequate, though I can well imagine certain implications, certain, ah—yes! it will do!

> *He concludes pompously, then attempts to smile furtively at the* WOMAN. *The* MAN *puts his hand on her shoulder: it is apparent he too is made uneasy somehow by this* WOMAN.

MAN: Come on now, if you'll just . . .

> *She stands compliantly, allows herself to be led to the table. The* PRIEST *paces round and round, trying in vain not to look at her, smiling foolishly each time their gazes chance to meet.*

That's it. Here. On the table . . .

PRIEST: Oops! Careful! These things!

*Clutching nervously, solicitously, for the fruit bas-
ket, he knocks it off the table.*

Oh! I'm sorry! Good heavens! It's just that I, that I, I
was only trying to . . .

The MAN *brushes the* PRIEST *aside gently, sets the
pitcher, glasses, and bread on the floor, poking the
knife into the bread. The* PRIEST *scrambles about
self-consciously, retrieving the fruit. The* WOMAN
*stands impassively in front of the table, waiting for
instructions. The* MAN *hesitates before lifting her up
on the table, stares coldly at her a moment.*

MAN: You're enjoying this, aren't you, damn you!

She smiles demurely.

PRIEST: (*still picking up fruit*) Uff, that's it, I think, yes
. . . sorry, I, uh, well, shouldn't cry over spilt—how
does that go? well, heh heh, doesn't matter . . .

The MAN *lifts the* WOMAN *up on the table. The*
PRIEST *watches, rapt.*

MAN: All right, there you are . . .

*She sits on the edge of the table, her hands folded in
her lap. The* PRIEST *advances awkwardly.*

Not yet.

The MAN *helps the* WOMAN *get stretched out, lifts her feet up on the table, then turns to the* PRIEST, *startling him.*

PRIEST: Well!

Awkward pause.

All ready, eh?

He laughs self-consciously, licks his lips.

Well. Well.

He crosses behind the table, stares a moment at the WOMAN *stretched out lengthwise in front of him, then impulsively bends and gives her a hasty pecking kiss on the cheek. He looks up guiltily at the* MAN.

I just felt I ought to do that.

MAN: That's all right.

PRIEST: It just seemed like, you know, the proper thing.

MAN: Sure.

PRIEST: First.

MAN: Are you sure you know what you're doing?

PRIEST: Oh, yes, yes! Of course! I think so, yes. I have manuals, that is, not with me, but I—of course! certainly!

A brief but uncomfortable pause.

MAN: (*to the* WOMAN) All right, lift your knees . . .

She does so.

Feet apart.

She complies. She smiles faintly, a bit nervously perhaps, sometimes watching one of the two men, sometimes not.

(*To the* PRIEST) All right, she's looking at you.

PRIEST: Thank you. But . . . but you needn't have . . .

The MAN *shrugs. The* PRIEST *circles the table again, arriving finally at the end facing the* WOMAN's *feet. He hesitates, makes a little motion as though crossing himself, then attempts to crawl up on the table. His cassock binds him.*

Excuse, me, would you, uh, would you mind . . .?

The MAN *shrugs again, steps behind the* PRIEST, *and shoving from the rear, boosts him up on the table. The* PRIEST *tumbles awkwardly between the* WOMAN's *legs.*

Thank you—*oops!* Ooh, sorry! beg your pardon! good grief!

He is making every effort, in his clumsiness, not to touch her, giggling uncontrollably all the while. His chains and pendants rattle in her skirts. She starts slightly, clasps her hands to her breast, but continues to smile placidly, innocently. The PRIEST, *with an apologetic grimace, tosses the chains and pendants over his shoulder.*

I . . . I can remove them, if you like . . .

MAN: It's all right. She doesn't mind.

PRIEST: Oh. Well, tell me. I'd be glad to . . .

> *Cautiously the* PRIEST *edges forward on his knees, then sits back on his heels. Diffidently, uncertainly, he plucks the* WOMAN's *skirts up to her knees, and one by one they tumble softly down, gathering in a heap around her thighs. The* MAN *observes impassively.*

Well. Heh heh. I guess we're almost . . .

> *He points a trembling finger in the general direction of her bodice.*

Er, excuse me, but do you mind if . . . if . . .?

MAN: No, I guess not.

> *The* MAN *opens the* WOMAN's *bodice and works it apart to expose her breasts. She smiles demurely up at him as he does so, then smiles at the* PRIEST *as the* MAN *withdraws.*

PRIEST: Oh! Well! Indeed! Thank you, that's very kind! It wasn't necessary, of course . . .

MAN: It's okay.

PRIEST: I mean, it was only . . . I . . .

MAN: I know. It helps.

PRIEST: Yes, that's what I meant.

He giggles.

I know why, but still it . . .

An awkward pause.

Well, um, they are quite lovely.

MAN: Yes, I think so.

PRIEST: So, ah, white!

MAN: Yes, she is fair.

PRIEST: Yes, fair, that's what I meant.

He giggles.

I've forgotten some of the words. Fair. Yes. I think we speak of marble.

MAN: Yes. And snow.

PRIEST: And snow! Hee hee, yes! But, ah, let's see, you would say, uh, plump, wouldn't you? Plump?

MAN: Well. Or just full.

PRIEST: Oh yes! Full! Fair and full! Heh heh . . .

MAN: And getting fuller every day.

PRIEST: How's that?

MAN: Her titties. They're getting bigger.

PRIEST: Oh yes! Of course! That's . . . that's not unusual, is it?

MAN: And they used to be pink around the nipples there. Pretty and pink. Now they're brown.

PRIEST: Oh! Hmm, yes, I see. Well. Well, I *like* them brown, it makes them so, so . . .

MAN: I like big titties. But I like pink ones better than brown ones.

PRIEST: But brown is so, so . . .

> *He licks his lips, hesitates, then reaches out gingerly, unsure of himself, and pinches one breast gently. The* WOMAN *watches, smiles. He giggles nervously and jiggles the breast a little.*

Cootchie-cootchie-coo!

> *He giggles, feeling wicked, his eyes half-closed, his head squeezed down between his shoulders. She smiles decorously. He jiggles the other one.*

Cootchie-cootchie—

MAN: Oh, come on! Let's get on with it!

PRIEST: (*reddening, thoroughly abashed, his voice faint and dry, barely audible*) I'm sorry. Excuse me. I only . . .

MAN: I know, it's all right. But let's get it over with.

PRIEST: (*weakly*) . . . Thought it would help. Well. Well, I guess I might as well . . . as you say . . .

> *Timorously, he peers down under the skirts, pushing them back. He makes mumbly little noises as he*

delicately probes and touches, looks up apologeti-
cally toward the MAN *and* WOMAN *from time to*
time.

Well, ah, everything seems to be, that is, heh heh, as one
would expect, more or less expect . . .

MAN: Maybe you'd rather I left you alone—?

PRIEST: No! Oh no, no, no indeed! That would be altogether, I mean, there should be, there should be witnesses!

MAN: Yes, you're probably right.

PRIEST: Yes. Witnesses. (*Somewhat haughtily, yet giddily:*)
Of course, I'm right!

MAN: All right, I'll watch then.

PRIEST: That's how it should be.

The MAN *stands behind the table to observe, as the*
PRIEST, *bracing himself for his task, edges forward*
on his knees. The WOMAN *smiles demurely.*

These damned robes!

MAN: (*laughing sympathetically*) They're a problem!

PRIEST: You should only know!

MAN: I can tell.

PRIEST: Well. Ah. How am I doing?

MAN: Not bad. Hang on to it now. You're getting there. Can I hold the robes out of the way for you?

PRIEST: No! No, you mustn't! I . . . there! Aren't I—?

MAN: Yes. There you—woops! No, it's . . . yes, there! You have it now!

PRIEST: (*giggling nervously*) You understand . . . that is, ah, I'm not too accustomed, it's not my ordinary . . .

> *The* MAN *claps his hand on the* PRIEST'*s shoulder reassuringly.*

MAN: Sure, I know. You're doing just fine!

PRIEST: Well, thank you. Thank you. Really, you're a great help, I do appreciate it . . .

MAN: Forget it.

PRIEST: No, really, I want you to know. I mean, this situation, it's all rather, for you, I mean . . .

> *A thoughtful pause.*

And if she . .   ? If it were really her . . . ?

MAN: How's that?

PRIEST: Oh, nothing, I, I . . .

> *He gazes with gathering awe and excitement down on the* WOMAN, *who remains as placid as ever.*

It's just that I've often, that this has all happened before, in a way, that I've been here, I've imagined, I've approached, that I've often had dreams . . .

MAN: Fantasies . . .

PRIEST: Yes, call them that if you wish . . .

MAN: You taught me the word just today.

PRIEST: . . . Or aspirations. Mythogenetic visions. Sacred really. A kind of devotion. Yes. It's a way, you know, of apprehending the transcendence, I've read about it, of trying to . . .

> *The* PRIEST's *excitement augments. The* MAN *watches closely the scene of the proximate encounter.*

She. Yes, it might be. She. It is always "she." It has always been "she." The impossible illimitable unapproachable "she." But to dream, to make of that "she" a "her," you see, to become at once substantive and verb, and so not only transform "she" to a knowable "her" but at the same time transubstantiate the self, yes! Substantive and verb! Matter and spirit! Oh my God, I've got the sweet taste of trinities in my mouth!

MAN: Say! You're doing all right down here, too!

PRIEST: It's—*AH!*

> *The* WOMAN *catches her breath, her eyes open widely, and she arches her back slightly, then relaxes, as before.*

Oh! Well, good heavens! I think, I think I've done it! Or did it! I . . . can you tell?

MAN: (*peering closely*) Hmmm. Almost . . .

> *He puts his arms around the* PRIEST *and pulls him in deeper.*

Just a little push, and . . . *there!*

PRIEST: (*gasping*) *Ooo!* yes! oh God in heaven! it's all warm! and wet! and . . .

> *He pauses, registering astonishment.*

But wait! There was, you said, it—there was no resistance! I don't understand! You told me she—? Why, she's—*she's been penetrated before!*

MAN: (*turning away*) Well . . .

PRIEST: I mean, there may be some things I don't know about breeding, not many, some, but our lives are not that sheltered, maidenheads I have had converse with! And I can tell you, this woman—!

> *The* MAN *walks away from them, returning to his stool. He sits with his back to them, a smile flickering on his lips. The* PRIEST, *still coupled with the* WOMAN, *pulls himself as erect as possible, under the circumstances.*

Now, see here! Why didn't you simply deny the story when I came? Why this ridiculous charade? Don't you realize how you've imposed on me, how you've imposed on the Church, I don't even mention this young woman here, I left my duties, my studies, my affairs of state, and what I want to know is—*oh!*

He giggles. To the WOMAN:

Stop that!

MAN: (*turning back to them*) Excuse me?

PRIEST: Nothing. She—I'd, uh, forgotten they could do that, it's—*oh!* Again! It's, heh heh, well! it's—*oh!* just like . . .

MAN: Like another mouth . . .

PRIEST: (*giggling*) Yes! I don't remember if that's—well, that's normal, isn't it? I mean, yes, I'm sure it—*oooh!*

The MAN *has turned away. The* PRIEST *glances at each of them in turn, then wriggles a little deeper into the* WOMAN. *He is perspiring freely and his ordinarily pale face is flushed.*

Listen. Perhaps I can still, eh, it was a nasty trick, but perhaps I can still forgive you. Yes, that is, as long as I'm already, ah, already here, so to speak, could—*oh!* heh heh!—I mean, this far, since I'm this far, would you mind, you know, would it be all right if . . .?

MAN: Sure. Go ahead.

PRIEST: Well, not if you really don't want me to.

MAN: I said it was all right.

PRIEST: It won't bother her . . . in her, you know, condition?

MAN: No, go ahead. She's all yours.

PRIEST: (*pushing the heavy folds of his cassock out of the way, leaning down gratefully into the woman, giggling softly*) Well, that's . . . that's white of you . . . quite . . . uh . . . white . . .

> *The* WOMAN *smiles at him, as before. The* MAN, *turned away, sighs. The* PRIEST, *settling himself, lays his head dreamily in the* WOMAN'*s breasts, nuzzling them, his tall pointed miter pressed down on her placid face. He mutters softly.*

Did I say white? Fair, yes. And brown. Mmmm. Really, you know, you're quite lucky. Yes. That she's safe from the, ah, from the law, I mean. Would've been a . . . waste. Quite nice, brown. Pink, too. They're still pink. Here and there. Pink and brown. And red. Rosy red. Fair. Pimples though. Little pimples.

MAN: Those are glands.

PRIEST: Glands. Yes. Of course they are. That's what I meant.

MAN: They keep the nipples soft.

PRIEST: Yes, of course. Soft. Mmmm. Strange we should speak of marble. Too many statues. We grow up with too many statues. Too many . . .

> *Slowly, smiling dreamily, he begins to undulate between her legs.*

. . . Statues. Marble. Ivory. Truth in marble, though. Yes. It lasts. Like the word. The letter. The letter of the law. Imagine. The soft letter of the soft law . . .

He giggles softly, irreverently, then begins to work faster and faster, his eyes opening and glazing over, his breath heaving, muttering monosyllables, his hands nervous on her body. Then, gradually, he slows. Finally, he stops.

These robes are warm.

MAN: Would you like me to help you off with them?

PRIEST: (*with effort, short of breath*) Good heavens, no!

MAN: But if it'd help . . .

PRIEST: Don't be impertinent!

His head is still resting on the WOMAN's breasts, his pointed hat on her smiling face. The MAN picks up an apple from the floor, polishes it on his pants, returning to his stool.

It was better when I thought . . . when it might be . . . might have been . . . she.

Pause.

Still . . . here we are . . .

Pause.

And she does have lovely brown . . . titties . . .

Pause. He seems to be falling asleep on her breasts.

Titties . . .

Pause. Less audibly:

Tummy . . .

Pause. Less audibly still:

Bottom . . . bottom . . .

Pause. A whisper:

Pussy . . .

Longer pause. Gradually, as this continues, he begins to undulate again.

And soft . . . mmm . . . flexuous . . .

MAN: (*eating the apple*) How's that?

PRIEST: Flexuous. Supple. Responsive . . .

MAN: You're fond of words.

PRIEST: (*now moving faster and faster*) Yes, I like words. Oh yes, words, the good old words! (*He opens his eyes.*) Resilient! Elastic! Velutinous! I could teach you some you've never—ah!—never heard before!

MAN: (*around the apple*) You already have.

PRIEST: Yes! Tractable! Sericeous! Edematous! Oooo! (*Faster and faster.*) Buttery! Lubricous! Oleaginous!

MAN: (*faintly disgusted*) Please!

The PRIEST is past hearing him—faster and faster he works, rearing his head up, spilling words, staring greedily down on the WOMAN, who smiles demurely back at him.

PRIEST: Viscous! Uff! Unguentiferous! Oh! Heavenly! Diabolical! Whoo! Pulchri—*oh!* Yes! Lubricous! I said that! Thermogenic! There's one! Febrifacient! Oh, it's good! Pungent! Concupiscible! Ah! Omophagous! Oh! I should say! Paludal! Poo!

> *Gradually, he tapers off, the words fading to an inaudible breathless muttering. He slows. He stops. He is gasping for breath. He looks dizzily over at the* MAN, *who is staring off, munching the apple. He is nearly voiceless.*

MAN: Nothing seems . . .

PRIEST: Nothing seems to happen.

MAN: I know.

PRIEST: It's . . . it's strange. It seems always about to, but finally . . . finally it doesn't.

> *The* MAN *stands, tosses the apple core away. The* PRIEST *watches him with narrowing eyes. Then he looks down at the* WOMAN, *back at the* MAN.

So . . . so that's it!

MAN: That's it. Some of it . . .

PRIEST: (*to the* WOMAN) So that's it . . . !

> *Suddenly, in a frenzy, clenching his teeth, grasping her angrily by the hips, he drives into her with furious abandon. Faster and faster he plunges, grunting out angry monosyllables. Tears come to his*

eyes. His lips draw back. Then, gradually, he slows again. Finally, he collapses limply over her, wheezing, snorting, whimpering.

MAN: Well?

PRIEST: (*sobbing*) Nothing.

MAN: Now you know.

PRIEST: (*still wheezing and snorting*) I've . . . I've done everything, haven't I? Have I . . . have I left anything out?

MAN: No. That's it. You can see what it's been like for me.

PRIEST: It's . . . it's not fair.

MAN: I gave it up altogether months ago.

PRIEST: It's unnatural, a . . . a—hoo! I'm exhausted!— it's a, well, a profanation!

MAN: I was afraid it might be something catching.

PRIEST: There's probably a name for it . . . a penance to . . . foo! . . . I'm too weak to think . . . !

There is a long recuperative pause. The MAN *sits and waits. The* PRIEST *finally, with great effort, coughing and gasping still, lifts himself off the* WOMAN's *bosom, glares down at her.*

You realize, my dear . . . that this is . . . huf! . . . this is no laughing matter!

She smiles up at him.

Now, stop that!

She stops smiling, gazes serenely up at him.

This is nothing to smile about, confound it! I am entirely serious! The plain fact is, you can be charged with witchcraft!

She smiles.

Witchcraft!

She stops smiling, watches him serenely.

The punishment for that little offense, my dear, is the stake!

She smiles.

Stop smiling, damn it! I said, *the stake!*

She stops smiling etc.

Do you know what we do to witches, my pet? We strip them naked and chase them through the public places with whips!

She smiles.

Whips, damn it! Whips! With barbs!

> *She stops smiling etc. The* MAN *stands, growing concerned. The* PRIEST *is hoarse but determined. Sometimes he is almost inaudible, sometimes he is almost screaming. As he harangues, he begins once more to move inside the* WOMAN, *gradually increasing momentum.*

And then we—uf!—pluck out their eyes and—ah!—
pull out their nails, yes, and stick pins, pins in the raw finger-
tips! Hah! Ram a flaming—oh!—a flaming broomstick
up their arse!

She smiles.

Damn you, *up the arse!* Slivers and all!

She stops smiling etc. The MAN *watches intently.*

And then—ah!—we—oh!—I forget! Uff! We stick
their legs in wooden boots! yes! jam 'em to jelly!
yes! throw them in dungeons! oh my stars!

*He is thrusting faster and faster, and seems to have
lost all control. His head wags violently from side
to side like a puppet's.*

Dungeons! Ah! Excrement! Ay ay! Hideous vermin!
Ah! Private parts! Whooey! And then we—oh!
Burning oil! Strangle them!

*He is all atremble, eyes rolling open and exposing
only the whites, mouth agape, spittle dribbling
down his chin. The* MAN *watches anxiously.*

And then, then we—ah!—tie—uff!—cut off their
—oh!—ashes! please! we—oh! dear God! crush! oh!
oh dear! AAAHH!*

The PRIEST *collapses suddenly on top of her body.
He is gagging, trembling violently, eyes rolled
back. The* MAN *rushes up.*

MAN: (*excitedly*) Did you do it?

PRIEST: (*faintly, choking*) No . . . no . . .

MAN: Oh, that's too bad. I thought for a minute there . . .

PRIEST: (*gagging, sobbing*) No . . . my heart . . . my heart, I think . . . I think I . . . almost had a . . . a stroke!

MAN: I think you'd better give it up.

PRIEST: Yes . . . I think I nearly . . . had a stroke . . .

> *Pause. No one moves. From the* WOMAN's *breast, the* PRIEST *focusing with difficulty, looks up toward the* MAN.

Please . . . I know it's wrong . . . I shouldn't give up . . . but . . . could you—? . . . I'm so tired, so very tired . . . can you help me? . . . I don't think I can even . . .

MAN: You mean you want help getting out?

PRIEST: Yes . . . please . . . oh! hurry! I think she's— please! I think she's biting me . . . !

MAN: Oh oh! Sure! Here!

> *He grasps the* PRIEST *round the middle from behind and pulls him away from the* WOMAN. *The* PRIEST *screams horribly, doubles forward like a jackknife springing shut, spins, and tumbles down behind the table, jerking and twisting about down there, as the*

MAN *and* WOMAN *both duck and throw up their arms, as though warding something off—*

Oops! Look out!

The PRIEST *groans profoundly, commences to weep softly. The* WOMAN *wipes her face and bosom delicately with a handkerchief.*

I'm sorry, I . . . I forgot to tell you . . .

The sobs fade to gasps, heavy breathing.

Are you all right?

PRIEST: (*stretched out, faintly*) Yes. Now. I think so.

MAN: It was my fault. I sort of forgot to mention that part.

PRIEST: Very strange . . .

MAN: Still, it would have happened anyway.

PRIEST: (*distantly*) Probably . . .

MAN: It always does.

PRIEST: Just like that? When you . . . after you . . . ?

MAN: Yes, you have it. And . . . well . . . there's something more . . .

PRIEST: More!

MAN: Yes, you see—

PRIEST: I don't want to hear about it.

Pause. Distantly:

There must be a precedent. I must go look it up.

MAN: (*looking down on the* PRIEST) There's no hurry.

PRIEST: It's late, after all. Much has happened.

MAN: Think of your heart . . .

PRIEST: I remember a terrible cave I was in as a boy . . .

Pause.

They said there was a bear . . .

Pause.

A wild bear . . .

Pause.

And if there are no precedents?

Pause.

We shall, I suppose, create them . . .

Pause.

I must go.

Pause.

Yes, I must go . . .

Pause.

Goodbye . . .

Longer pause.

Please . . . can you . . . could you give me a hand?

The MAN *helps the* PRIEST *to sit upright. The* PRIEST *is haggard, looks much older, eyes glazed and staring.*

MAN: I'm afraid you've stained your robes.

PRIEST: (*vaguely*) No doubt.

MAN: It'll wash out.

PRIEST: It always does.

MAN: Some wine maybe . . . ?

PRIEST: If you don't mind.

The MAN *inspects the two glasses on the floor, selects one, rinses it out with a little wine, pours it full and hands it to the* PRIEST. *The* PRIEST *accepts it absently, gulps it down greedily.*

More!

The MAN *refills the glass, and again the* PRIEST *empties it.*

Ahh!

MAN: More?

PRIEST: No.

MAN: Are you sure?

PRIEST: (*irritably*) Of course, I'm sure. (*More gently:*) Thank you.

> *He begins the struggle to get to his feet. The* MAN *rushes to help.*

MAN: Easy!

PRIEST: I'm all right! Leave me alone!

> *He falls to the floor.*

MAN: (*helping the* PRIEST *back up*) You're still weak . . .

PRIEST: I should have thought about my heart.

MAN: You had me worried.

PRIEST: I nearly had a stroke.

MAN: You had . . . quite an orgasm!

PRIEST: (*smiling weakly*) Did I? I can only vaguely remember . . .

MAN: (*trying to cheer him up*) It was . . . damned impressive!

PRIEST: (*distantly*) All these years . . .

MAN: It was . . .

PRIEST: Copious?

MAN: That's the word!

> *Reflective pause.*

PRIEST: You did this to me on purpose!

MAN: (*taken by surprise*) Did I? No, I mean, well, I . . .

PRIEST: You knew the law! You knew the law! Penetration, however slight, you knew that! It was a trick!

MAN: But it wasn't me, I—anyway, I needed your—

PRIEST: I nearly died!

MAN: I didn't realize you'd . . . you'd work so hard at it.

PRIEST: Hmmph! I am nothing if not thorough! But I just don't see . . .

MAN: Well, there's the . . . whatever it is she's growing . . .

PRIEST: Oh yes. Yes, that is a problem. I see. She's said nothing?

MAN: (*glancing uneasily toward the* WOMAN) Well, nothing I . . . uh, nothing I can really . . .

PRIEST: Hasn't said who . . . that is, how . . . ?

MAN: No, not . . . not directly . . .

PRIEST: Well, we shall find out for you. We have ways.

MAN: (*alarmed*) You won't hurt her!

PRIEST: Are you telling *me* what we will or will not do? We will do what we must! We are *going* to get to the bottom of this!

A rich husky cascade of laughter issues forth from beneath the WOMAN'*s skirts. Her* CUNT *speaks:*

CUNT: The bottom of it indeed! Going to kiss the Devil's unguentiferous oleaginous ass, are you, father?

PRIEST: (*turning in surprise toward the* WOMAN) I beg your pardon?

CUNT: Well, I'm not surprised! You couldn't tell it apart from God's tit if we provided you with survey maps, could you, priest?

The PRIEST, *astounded, searches about frantically for the source of the voice: under the table, in his own robes, etc. As the* CUNT *speaks, the* MAN *gradually relaxes, any hostility he might have displayed toward the* PRIEST *melting away. It is all out in the open now, and he looks to the educated man for help in resolving his domestic crisis.*

God's fair full brown pink velutinous omophagous tit!

PRIEST: But who—? Where—?

MAN: It's her cunt. It talks. You see, I thought you . . . it's why I . . .

CUNT: I use your language, having failed with my own.

PRIEST: (*bending toward the* CUNT, *but keeping his distance*) You mean—!

CUNT: Why are you surprised? It's nothing new! You have witnesses!

MAN: You can see the lips move if you get close enough.

PRIEST: My word!

CUNT: No, mine! And the word is flux, the bloody simpliciter flux!

MAN: I thought I saw a tongue once, but I'm not sure . . .

CUNT: Trouble is, you boys get misled by the rigidity, secundum quid, of your own organs.

PRIEST: (*edging closer, starting to giggle*) Well, bless my heart! A talking . . . I mean, what would be the—?

CUNT: You work up a hard-on and like it so much you call it a system, but you're afraid of orgasm and call it death!

PRIEST: Yes: *vagina qui verba facit* . . .

MAN: (*for whom all this is no longer funny*) I thought you could help me . . .

CUNT: Now, the soft letter of the soft law, that was something else, you nearly broke through there, might've been a different story . . .

PRIEST: (*edging closer*) *Loquax. Vagina lo*—

MAN: Watch out you don't get too close there! Last time I bent down like that she pissed in my eye!

PRIEST: (*drawing back*) Really—!

CUNT: But then you had to stuff all those horrid monuments up my gullet! Sericeous! Febrifacient! Worse than the flaming broomstick, my God!

MAN: Said she was baptizing me!

The PRIEST *breaks into sniggering laughter.*

CUNT: (*continuing over their exchanges*) Your prick may be hard as a rock, priest, but it's as cold as one, too!

MAN: (*angry at the laughter*) That's sacrilege, isn't it?

PRIEST: Eh? Oh! Hmmph! Yes . . . ahem! But why didn't you tell me in the first place?

CUNT: It's murder, that's what it is!

MAN: I was afraid you wouldn't believe me. I had to wait for her to give herself away.

CUNT: You've got about as much chance of fucking the world alive with that theological position of yours as you have of lighting a fire with mud!

MAN: (*breaking down*) I didn't know where else to turn. I couldn't keep it to myself any longer! You've read things, I thought . . .

PRIEST: Hmmm. Has she . . . ? Has it . . . ?

CUNT: That old brute with the beard must have started it when he went up the mountain, we've been living in the Stone Age ever since!

PRIEST: I mean, how long . . . ?

MAN: The talking? About four months now. The fucking problem, ever since we got married. I thought it was my fault. But the talking . . . well, ever since . . .

He indicates her belly. The PRIEST *mulls things over, circling about the* WOMAN.

CUNT: He and his letter of the law! What a desperation!

MAN: She woke me up one night. Her cunt did, I mean.

CUNT: Only man could hang himself with glossaries, blow his brains out with metaphors!

MAN: She said she wanted to tell me a story.

PRIEST: A story?

CUNT: If you ask them what genesis is, they'll tell you it's a book on jurisprudence.

MAN: It was a history of cunts, she said. A new history of cunts. Something like that. She said she'd had enough assaults on the world by the old sausage gods and their abdominal mother fucking . . .

CUNT: Abominable.

PRIEST: Yes, abominable . . . er, eh, good grief!

CUNT: He wanted to put me in a circus. Still, that's not the worst idea he had.

PRIEST: Weren't you rather surprised?

MAN: You damn right! Scared the shit out of me! I thought sure a devil had crawled up her. I mean, a cunt can't talk, can it?

CUNT: Do you think it's the way I want it? Do you think I'm happy?

MAN: It's not her fault, I thought. My wife's, I mean. It's just that something's got inside there, and so, well, I thought you'd know what it was and how to get it out.

CUNT: Sometimes I yearn for the old simplicities, too, you know. Sometimes I think it's not fair.

PRIEST: It's possible, that is, I've read . . . though I've never—eh, was she suddenly that large, like she is now, or did she grow?

MAN: She grew.

CUNT: Why me? I ask. I've got an appetite for foaming floods of boiling seed like any other cunt, why have I got to be the saint?

PRIEST: Well then . . .

MAN: You mean . . . but a devil could start small and grow, too, couldn't he?

CUNT: Such a clumsy bastard! He knows what he wants to do, but still hasn't been able to figure out what his own face looks like.

PRIEST: Has your urination been impeded? Have you had regular bowel movements?

MAN: No, *I'm* all right, it's only her . . .

CUNT: Can the substance embrace its shadow? Can the mirror fuck its image? No, it's not his fault . . .

PRIEST: But awhile ago, you, eh, you had some difficulty achieving . . .

MAN: You mean about getting it up to lay her for you? I was just pretending. I wanted you to find out for your—

PRIEST: (*bristling again*) Pretending! You mean you made me suffer that . . . that indignity—!

CUNT: It'll wash out, it always does.

MAN: It wasn't just my idea. That's the way she wanted it. I was afraid she wouldn't talk if . . .

CUNT: You've got to get the feel of it, father. In the old days, they did it through the ear, the velutinous oleaginous ear, but the times are desperate and the ear is calloused from all the violations . . .

MAN: (*desperately*) See? You see? She goes on and on like that! All night long! All day long!

CUNT: We have to stir the senses, grab you where it hurts! Any penetration, however slight, is a bloody business!

MAN: I mean, goddamn it, I've had enough! I work hard, the world is tough, I need a place to relax, somebody to help me find a moment's peace! I deserve it! How can she understand how it is for me? I mean, I care for her, I respect her, I love her—but we all have our work, we all have our place, and she has hers!

> There is the sound of a loud wet fart from beneath the WOMAN's skirts.

PRIEST: (*crossing himself*) God save us!

MAN: *You see!!!*

CUNT: Let those who have ears hear!

PRIEST: Now, that's quite enough!

MAN: I'M JUST NOT GONNA PUT UP WITH THIS KINDA SHIT AROUND MY HOUSE!!

CUNT: How did I get here, you ask? Poor circulation maybe, pathological hypostasis, it's happened before . . .

PRIEST: Isn't there some way of stopping it?

CUNT: A revolt in the promptuary . . .

MAN: I even told her, go away! Go away, if you want to! Piss in somebody else's eye, I told her. But she won't even go away!

CUNT: Listen to me! *Te oro, pater!* This is the wild bear speaking to you from the terrible cave!

> The PRIEST, *in a sudden desperate act, shoves his hand up the* WOMAN's *skirts:*

You can't fuck me with your old theological——*uck!*

> *Silence, except for the* PRIEST's *heavy breathing. He's a little shocked at what he's done.*

PRIEST: There . . . ! Hah!

MAN: (*uneasily*) I've tried that, you'd better . . .

PRIEST: Stopped it! Very good! But we have to work fast! We have to think! Have you noticed any unusual marks on her? Any extra teats?

MAN: Uh . . . she's apt to—

PRIEST: Listen to me! I can't keep it plugged up forever! Have any children disappeared? I need my books! There are precedents, yes, I'm sure of it, but— *YEEEOOOOWW!!!*

> *The* PRIEST *leaps up and down in pain, hand still caught under the skirts.*

Oh my God! Help! I can't get it out! I think she's eating me! Oh Holy Mother! Please! Mercy! It's terrible! Oh dear God!

> *Suddenly, he falls away. He stumbles in terror to the opposite side of the room from the* WOMAN, *wringing his hand, pressing it between his knees, etc., moaning with pain.*

CUNT: If you don't want to be enslaved, friend, you have to suffer . . .

MAN: I tried to warn you . . .

PRIEST: Burn her! She has to be burned!

CUNT: That's right, anything you don't understand, kill it, that's your road to salvation, your covenant with holy inertia! Kill and codify!

MAN: Burn her! But—!

PRIEST: No buts about it! There's not a moment to lose!

CUNT: You love to fog up the ether with your own hokum nimbi, debase the living world with phony mystifications sprung spookily from your geometries and glossolalias, but how you shy from something so simple as communication with your own gametes! Hey, I'm calling to your balls, boys!

MAN: But I'd hate to lose her! That way, anyway . . . !

PRIEST: I know. Do you think it's any easier for me? I have seen too many fires fed by the ooze of human fat in my time as it is! It's made a vegetarian out of me!

CUNT: An exemplary deprivation, father! Isn't that what you tell the little boys when you take them out in the forest? Liberation from their fatal attachments!

PRIEST: No, no, the lot of a priest is one of pain and suffering, it's not as people think—I mean, you've seen today . . .

CUNT: Oh, we know what you tell them, it's no big secret! You tell them Adam had a tail and that's what God made Eve out of!

PRIEST: THAT'S ENOUGH!

CUNT: Well, that explains the itch in your assholes, all right, but doesn't account for Eve's celebrated appetite . . .

PRIEST: WE *CAN* STOP IT, DAMN YOU! WE *MUST* STOP IT!

The PRIEST *grabs up the loaf of bread with the knife in it, and with a sweep of his arm, hurls the bread off the blade. A momentary shocked pause.*

CUNT: Don't be sure it's so easy, father. One never knows where the wind blows, or whither the spirit next—

PRIEST: Think of her as a host! It'll be easier that way! She must be liberated from this demon!

CUNT: Ah, the unending hope for the diabolical! I tell you, you show me a *deus et diabolus*, and I'll show you a dirty old man trying to bugger his own brown pink marble fair full snowy rosy red ass!

PRIEST: *You fiend!*

He lunges forward with the knife, but the MAN *restrains him.*

MAN: *No! Please! Wait—!*

CUNT: Why do you fear a Second Coming when you haven't yet heard the announcement for the First? Why do you worship the sacred when nothing, not even diffusion or your own self-deceit, is profane?

PRIEST: (*turning viciously on the* MAN) Are you part of it, too? Are you under its spell?

MAN: (*withdrawing in fright*) No! No, I only . . . !

CUNT: You have turned law into iconolatry, letters into pillories!

The PRIEST *whirls on the* WOMAN *and, muttering some paternoster to himself, holds the blade high over her belly.*

Do you think you can stay the moving spirit in an alphabet?

PRIEST: IN GOD'S NAME . . . !

He plunges the knife into the WOMAN's *belly. The* WOMAN *and* MAN *utter short cries, the* MAN *rushing to the* WOMAN's *side.*

WOMAN: (*half-rising from the table, no longer smiling*) You . . . you have hurt me . . . !

CUNT: (*distantly*) You might as well try signing your name by pissing into a sandstorm . . . !

The CUNT's *voice trails off into a hollow fading sigh. The* WOMAN *collapses, cradled by the* MAN.

PRIEST: (*softly, brokenly*) It is done . . .

There is a prolonged silence. The PRIEST *says a few quiet words over the* WOMAN's *body, then makes his way, very slowly, toward the door. The* MAN *watches sullenly, then his expression slowly fades —his voice is heard, but his lips do not move:*

MAN'S PRICK: Now, we didn't need to do that . . .

Dispassionately, almost dreamily, the MAN *looks down in his pants whence the voice came. The* PRIEST *turns in alarm. Then his expression fades as*

*well, he too becomes placid, and in the same man-
ner as the* MAN's, *the* PRIEST's *voice is heard:*

PRIEST'S PRICK: We got carried away . . .

MAN'S PRICK: I feel so empty . . .

PRIEST'S PRICK: It's all emptying out . . .

MAN'S PRICK: Why is it we always become the thing we
struggle against?

PRIEST'S PRICK: Because of love . . .

Pause.

After all, there's something to be said for talking
cunts . . .

MAN'S PRICK: Yes, there's something to be said . . .

FADE

About the Author

ROBERT COOVER has been acclaimed by writers and critics as one of the strongest and most original voices in American fiction. His first novel, *The Origin of the Brunists*, was the winner of the 1966 William Faulkner Award for the best first novel of that year. In 1968 he wrote the highly praised novel, *The Universal Baseball Association, J. Henry Waugh, Prop.* In 1969 he published a collection of short stories entitled *Pricksongs & Descants*, and made a documentary film, *On a Confrontation in Iowa City*. Mr. Coover is married and the father of three children. He is presently at work on his third novel.